WILLIAMS-SONOMA

New American Cooking

The Southwest

GENERAL EDITOR **Chuck Williams**

RECIPES AND TEXT **Kathi Long**

FOOD PHOTOGRAPHY **Leigh Beisch**

TIME
LIFE
BOOKS

New Ameri

The Pacific Northwest

The

California

The Southwest

can Cooking

Heartland

New England

The South

Table of **Contents**

Introduction

Growing up in Ohio never prepared me for the Southwest. I moved to New Mexico in the mid-1970s, and suddenly found myself looking up at the bluest skies I had ever seen. Not long after my arrival, I attended my first fiesta in Santa Fe, where I discovered a regional table that rendered my former Midwest world of meat and potatoes a distant memory. The downtown streets were lined with booths selling tamales plump with shredded pork and sheathed in a spicy sauce, and Native American fry bread wrapped around ground beef, cheese, and chiles. Vendors offering fajitas, green chile stew, and posole stood alongside competitors hawking honey-drenched sopaipillas, chiles rellenos, and big bowls of steaming pinto beans.

I soon learned that generations of local cooks had prepared these same dishes—dishes rooted in a cultural mix that forms the foundation not only of New Mexico cooking but of Southwest cuisine as a whole. Today, the kitchens of the region continue to honor these longstanding culinary traditions—traditions that have flourished here but have seldom taken root elsewhere in the country. Simply put, Southwest cooking, whether because of geography, ingredients, or carefully guarded recipes, has stayed close to home.

The Region Defined

The borders of the Southwest are simply drawn. New Mexico and Arizona, with their broken mesas, bold canyons, wide deserts, and bare, towering peaks, stand at its center. Southern Colorado, a land of high valleys, deep canyons, and flat plains, reaches its northern border at Colorado Springs. Finally, hot and dusty west Texas, a stretch of rolling plains, rough uplands, and tracts of great wilderness, travels as far east as Wichita Falls and San Antonio and as far south as the Mexican border.

Water, or rather the lack of it, has long bound together these four Southwest states. They are all home to large arid and semiarid expanses, and until the early twentieth century and the beginnings of irrigation, these parched tracts saw only limited farming. Today, with a steady growth in population, especially in Arizona and New Mexico, the amount of irrigated land, fed by such regional rivers as the Rio Grande, the Pecos, the San Juan, and the Gila, has increased markedly, and with it has come a more varied agriculture and ranching profile.

In Arizona, beef and dairy cattle, lettuce, cauliflower, and broccoli are the primary focus of ranchers and farmers, while their New Mexico counterparts typically plant onions and potatoes, tend dairy cows, and produce smaller but significant harvests of piñon nuts, pinto beans, and chiles. Southern Colorado is sheep and cattle country; fields and orchards are planted with wheat, corn, and sugar beets and, to a lesser extent, melons, apples, and pears. Texas, one of the country's most important agricultural players, harvests corn, beans, tomatoes, and squashes, as well as citrus and other fruits and rice, and its sprawling ranches shelter herds of cattle and sheep.

A Varied Population

The culture of this dramatic, often harsh landscape has been largely shaped by Native Americans, Spaniards, Mexicans, and Anglos. By the eleventh century, the Pueblo Indians were thriving here, joined about a century later by the Apaches and Navajos. They grew corn, squashes, melons, and gourds and gathered wild fruits and vegetables, piñon nuts, and a variety of herbs and grasses for medicine and seasoning.

In the late 1530s, the first Spanish explorers arrived. Soon after, chiles and chocolate from Mexico and wheat, grapes, peaches, cherries, apples, plums, nuts, figs, dates, pomegranates, and spices from Europe became part of the Southwest pantry. Cattle, pigs, and sheep were also introduced, and the art of barbecue quickly followed. The long, porous border with Mexico brought new people and more new foods: tomatoes, avocados, vanilla, and turkeys.

A steady stream of Anglo trappers and traders made their way to the region in the mid-1800s, followed by large numbers of Anglo settlers who came to claim much of the region's grazing land. These newcomers introduced a wide range of European-style dishes, from heartwarming stews to homespun baked goods, that intermingled with the region's other culinary strands.

Fish tacos such as these (opposite) with pickled onions and chiles have become regional favorites. Ancho chiles, epazote, and tomatoes (above) represent the various cultural contributions to Southwest cooking.

Salsas are an integral part of Southwest cuisine. Tomatillo-Avocado Salsa (above) puts two key regional ingredients to delicious use. Texas barbecue inspires devotion in locals and visitors alike. This version (right), using baby back ribs, discloses that the secret's in the sauce. Flan (opposite), a favorite Southwestern dessert, demonstrates the region's Mexican roots.

The Southwest Kitchen

Today, Southwest cuisine distills all of these influences. New Mexico cooks have relied upon the traditions of a trio of kitchens, the Spanish, the Mexican, and the Pueblo Indian, to produce an earthy cuisine of blue-corn tortillas and *sopa de mariscos* (shellfish stew), *carne adobada* (spice-rubbed meat), and piñon-studded bread pudding.

Arizona cooks have likewise looked to Mexico for inspiration. The southern part of the state borrowed from the cooking of Sonora, which lies directly across the border, a culinary alliance that reveals itself in large, thin flour tortillas, the use of nopal cactus, and a menu of mildly spiced dishes. Elsewhere in the state, residents traditionally dine on Mexican chimichangas (deep-fried filled tortillas), menudo (tripe soup), and giant burritos, as well as the more staid ranch fare introduced by early cattlemen and other settlers from the Midwest and East Coast.

Cattle ranching played a critical role in the early economy of Texas

as well, a fact that has made bar-becued beef a mealtime standard in the state's homes. Fajitas, *cabrito* (barbecued goat), and tacos, dishes that showcase the tradition of Tex-Mex food—Mexican-American cooking in Texas—also are popular here, and the cowboy chuck wagon fare of the past lives on in bowl o' red, a version of chili con carne that is a specialty of San Antonio cooks. Immigrants from Scandinavia, Poland, Czechoslovakia, and Germany added their sausage-making and smokehouse-curing know-how to local kitchens.

Southern Colorado, which was settled later than its three Southwest neighbors, drew frontiersmen of French and Anglo origin, followed by miners and ranchers. Today their descendants who live along the border enjoy a cuisine much like that of northern New Mexico, with such fare as green and red chile sauces, sopaipillas, and rich, hearty stews. A bit north and west, in grazing country, robust ranch cuisine is served.

The Contemporary Table

Although Southwest cooking varies from New Mexico to Arizona, southern Colorado to west Texas, common elements link the tables. Informal, family-style dining is the rule throughout the region, along with a tradition-bound menu of dishes more keyed to comfort than elegance. A growing interest in first-rate ingredients is found all over the Southwest as well, as evidenced by the burgeoning roster of farmers' markets selling specialty produce and other pantry staples, from local honeys to artisanal cheeses.

Local cooks, both in homes and restaurants, recognize that Southwest cuisine has evolved over time, losing some of its rustic character and taking on some culinary sophistication in the process. But they also know what makes Southwest cooking a true regional fare: a respect for tradition, for what is local and seasonal, and an understanding of the history and rich cultural mix that is at its heart.

1 Starters, Soups & Salads

Many of the Southwest's favorite starters and soups—quesadillas concealing squash blossoms, ceviche fired with serrano chile and cooled with avocado, chorizo empanadas, blue-corn tamales, *sopa de lima*—reveal the profound influence of Mexican cuisine on the regional table. Salads, typically a mix of the new and the familiar, show up in first place, too, featuring both universal ingredients—beets, cabbage, tomatoes—and a basketful of regional ones—*nopales,* pumpkin seeds, Ruby grapefruit, jicama.

Squash Blossom Quesadillas

12 flour tortillas, each 7–8 inches (18–20 cm) in diameter

1½ cups (6 oz/185 g) shredded Monterey jack cheese

¾ cup (4 oz/125 g) crumbled *queso fresco* or mild feta cheese

leaves from 6 fresh epazote sprigs

4 large fresh *hoja santa* leaves, cut lengthwise into strips ½ inch (12 mm) wide

3 or 4 serrano chiles, roasted, peeled, and seeded *(page 138),* then thinly sliced on the extreme diagonal

18 squash blossoms, stems and pistils removed and cut crosswise into strips ½ inch (12 mm) wide

kosher salt to taste

Native Americans of the Southwest—especially the Zunis, who live in western New Mexico—have long eaten the delicate golden blossoms of squashes, the best of which come from zucchini (courgettes). Although they may be stuffed and deep-fried, the flowers are used here to add bright color and subtle flavor to the region's distinctive version of the grilled cheese sandwich. Try making these with homemade Flour Tortillas (page 86) for a special treat.

1. Preheat the oven to 350°F (180°C).

2. Sprinkle 6 of the tortillas evenly with both cheeses, the epazote leaves, the *hoja santa* strips, the chiles, and the squash blossom strips. Sprinkle with salt and place a second tortilla on top of each filled one, pressing down gently. Transfer the quesadillas to 2 ungreased baking sheets.

3. Bake the quesadillas until the cheese starts to melt, 4–5 minutes. Carefully flip the quesadillas over and continue to bake until the cheese is melted, about 4 minutes longer. Remove from the oven and slide the quesadillas onto a cutting board. Cut each round into 6 pieces. Transfer to a serving platter and serve immediately.

SERVES 6–8

NUTRITIONAL ANALYSIS PER SERVING
Calories 339 (Kilojoules 1,424); Protein 14 g; Carbohydrates 34 g; Total Fat 16 g; Saturated Fat 8 g; Cholesterol 37 mg; Sodium 532 mg; Dietary Fiber 2 g

Jicama, Carrot, and Red Cabbage Salad

DRESSING

1 tablespoon finely chopped shallot

1 teaspoon minced serrano chile

1½ tablespoons white wine vinegar

1 tablespoon fresh lime juice

1 tablespoon sugar

kosher salt to taste

⅓ cup (3 fl oz/80 ml) safflower oil

1 small jicama, about ¼ lb (125 g), peeled and julienned

1 carrot, peeled and julienned

¼ small head red cabbage, finely shredded

handful of sunflower or radish sprouts, root ends trimmed

On hot summer days, Southwest cooks, following the lead of their Mexican counterparts, sprinkle crisp sticks of chilled, raw tropical jicama with coarse salt, ground New Mexico chile, and fresh lime juice. Here, jicama joins carrots, red cabbage, and bright green sprouts in a colorful salad that makes a refreshing side dish for outdoor meals.

1. To make the dressing, in a small bowl, whisk together the shallot, chile, vinegar, lime juice, sugar, and salt. Whisk in the oil. Set the mixture aside for about 10 minutes to allow the flavors to blend. Taste and adjust the seasoning.

2. In a bowl, combine the jicama, carrot, cabbage, and sprouts. Toss thoroughly to distribute the ingredients evenly. Add the dressing, toss, and serve immediately.

SERVES 4

NUTRITIONAL ANALYSIS PER SERVING
Calories 210 (Kilojoules 882); Protein 1 g; Carbohydrates 12 g; Total Fat 18 g; Saturated Fat 2 g; Cholesterol 0 mg; Sodium 14 mg; Dietary Fiber 3 g

Nopales with Jicama and Pumpkin Seeds

8 or 9 large nopal cactus paddles, about 1½ lb (750 g) total weight

¼ cup (2 fl oz/60 ml) olive oil

kosher salt and freshly ground pepper to taste

⅓ cup (1½ oz/45 g) hulled pumpkin seeds

3 large navel oranges

1 jicama, about 1 lb (500 g), peeled and julienned

1 small red (Spanish) onion, slivered

¼ cup (⅓ oz/10 g) coarsely chopped fresh cilantro (fresh coriander)

3 tablespoons toasted pumpkin seed oil

DRESSING

3 or 4 pickled jalapeño chiles, stems removed, plus 2 tablespoons of the juice

pinch of sugar

kosher salt to taste

⅓ cup (3 fl oz/80 ml) safflower oil

Exotic though they may seem, *nopales*, the pads of the prickly pear cactus, have an appealing color and flavor reminiscent of green beans. When preparing them, handle with care, using a thick towel or padded glove to protect your hands.

1. Position a rack in the upper third of the oven and preheat to 400°F (200°C). Line a baking sheet with aluminum foil.

2. Working with 1 cactus paddle at a time, and using a large knife, cut off the entire outside edge of the paddle, including the end where it was cut from the plant. Then, cut off the thorny nodes. Cut the paddles horizontally into strips ½ inch (12 mm) wide. In a bowl, combine the strips, olive oil, salt, and pepper. Pour onto the prepared baking sheet.

3. Roast until the strips are "dry" and the edges are slightly crisp, 20–25 minutes. Set aside to cool.

4. To make the dressing, in a blender, combine the chiles and juice, sugar, salt, and safflower oil. Purée until smooth. Set aside.

5. To toast the pumpkin seeds, in a small frying pan over medium-high heat, toast the seeds, stirring, until they begin to pop and are plump and lightly golden, about 3 minutes. Pour onto a plate to cool.

6. Working with 1 orange at a time, cut a slice off the top and bottom to expose the flesh. Stand the orange upright and thickly cut off the peel in strips to expose the flesh. Holding the orange over a large bowl, cut along either side of each section, letting it drop into the bowl.

7. In a bowl, combine the cactus strips, orange sections, jicama, onion, and cilantro and mix gently. Pour the dressing over the mixture and toss to combine. Divide among individual plates. Sprinkle with the pumpkin seeds and drizzle with the pumpkin seed oil. Serve at once.

SERVES 6

NUTRITIONAL ANALYSIS PER SERVING
Calories 357 (Kilojoules 1,499); Protein 3 g; Carbohydrates 24 g; Total Fat 29 g; Saturated Fat 4 g; Cholesterol 0 mg; Sodium 153 mg; Dietary Fiber 6 g

Cacti of all kinds dot the deserts of the Southwest, flourishing where other life withers under a relentless sun. When they bloom in the spring, they punctuate the landscape with colorful flowers that surprise the uninitiated. But even the eye-catching blossoms fail to convince most outlanders to eat any part of these prickly plants.

The Pueblo Indians have always known better. Long before others came to settle in the Southwest, these original residents were harvesting the big, flat paddles, or joints, and plump, oval fruits of the nopal, or prickly pear, cactus. They cooked and ate the fleshy joints and dried the fruits, which they ground and used as a sweetener.

Today, Southwest cooks use the paddles, or *nopales,* as a vegetable in salsas, stews, and salads; grilled; and cooked with eggs. Locals claim that they taste like a cross between green beans and okra with a touch of asparagus and a light citrus note. Like okra, they can become mucilaginous over heat unless cooked only a short time or blanched before using.

The egg-shaped fruit, with flesh ranging from white, pink, and yellow to orange and red, travels under

Nopal **Cactus**

many names: prickly pear, cactus pear, Indian fig, Barbary fig, and the Spanish *tuna.* Cooks use it as they do other fruits, principally in sweet and savory sauces, in compotes, and to make marmalade and jam. Prickly pears are also wonderful eaten out of hand, but care must be taken— thick gloves and judicious handling— to avoid a palm full of tiny spines.

Chorizo Empanadas with Ancho Chile Sauce

DOUGH

2 cups (10 oz/315 g) all-purpose (plain) flour

¾ teaspoon kosher salt

6 tablespoons (3 oz/90 g) chilled unsalted butter, cut into 6 pieces

6 tablespoons (3 oz/90 g) lard, bacon fat, or vegetable shortening

4–5 tablespoons (2–2½ fl oz/ 60–75 ml) ice water

SAUCE

3 ancho chiles

1 tablespoon roasted garlic (page 92)

2 tablespoons cider vinegar

1 cup (8 oz/250 g) chilled unsalted butter, cut into 8 pieces

kosher salt to taste

FILLING

2 tablespoons olive oil

½ white onion, finely chopped

2 cloves garlic, minced

1 teaspoon cumin seed, toasted (page 141)

½ teaspoon dried Mexican oregano

½ teaspoon freshly ground canela or ¼ teaspoon ground cinnamon

½ lb (250 g) bulk chorizo

1 egg white, lightly beaten with ¼ teaspoon water

1 whole egg, lightly beaten with 1 tablespoon heavy (double) cream

½ cup (2½ oz/75 g) crumbled queso fresco or queso añejo

1. To make the dough, in a food processor, combine the flour and salt and pulse to mix. Add the butter and the lard or other fat and process until the mixture resembles coarse crumbs. Add the water, 1 tablespoon at a time, until the mixture comes together. Turn out onto plastic wrap, shape into a disk, wrap, and refrigerate for 1 hour.

2. To make the sauce, in a small frying pan over medium-high heat, toast the chiles, turning once, until fragrant, 1–2 minutes. Immerse in hot water for 30 minutes. Drain, reserving the water, and discard the stems. In a blender, combine the chiles and ½ cup (4 fl oz/125 ml) of the soaking water and purée until smooth. If too thick, add a little more water, then pass through a medium-mesh sieve and reserve.

3. To make the filling, in a frying pan over medium-high heat, warm the olive oil. Add the onion and garlic and sauté until softened, 3–4 minutes. Add the cumin, oregano, and canela and cook for 1 minute. Crumble in the chorizo and cook until browned, 4–5 minutes. Drain in a sieve.

4. Preheat the oven to 425°F (220°C). Line a baking sheet with parchment (baking) paper. On a lightly floured work surface, roll out the dough ⅛ inch (3 mm) thick. Using a 4½-inch (11.5-cm) round cookie cutter, cut out as many rounds as possible. Reroll the scraps and cut out additional rounds. You should have 16 rounds. Place 1 tablespoon of the filling in the center of each round. Brush the edges with the egg white and fold in half. With floured fork tines, press the edges together to seal. Place on the prepared baking sheet and brush generously with the egg-cream mixture. Bake until golden brown, about 20 minutes. Let rest for 10 minutes.

5. Finish the sauce: In a saucepan over low heat, warm the ancho purée, roasted garlic, and vinegar. Add the butter, 2 pieces at a time, whisking well after each addition. Season with salt.

6. Top the empanadas with the sauce and cheese, then serve.

MAKES 16 EMPANADAS; SERVES 4

NUTRITIONAL ANALYSIS PER EMPANADA
Calories 368 (Kilojoules 1,546); Protein 7 g; Carbohydrates 17 g; Total Fat 31 g; Saturated Fat 15 g; Cholesterol 77 mg; Sodium 288 mg; Dietary Fiber 1 g

Blue Corn and Green Chile Tamales

Blue cornmeal, a signature Southwestern ingredient, imparts a beautiful blue-gray color and earthy taste to these tamales, which are filled with New Mexico's famed green chiles.

FILLING

2 tablespoons olive oil

½ white onion, finely chopped

2 cloves garlic, minced

¼ teaspoon dried Mexican oregano

3 or 4 New Mexico green chiles (about 9 oz/280 g total), roasted, peeled, and seeded *(page 138),* then chopped (about ⅔ cup/4 oz/125 g)

kosher salt to taste

MASA

1 cup (5 oz/155 g) stone-ground blue cornmeal

1 cup (5 oz/155 g) tamale-grind or stone-ground yellow cornmeal

1 teaspoon baking powder

1 teaspoon kosher salt

¾ cup (6 oz/185 g) lard or vegetable shortening

1¼ cups (10 fl oz/310 ml) chicken stock, heated

3 oz (90 g) dried corn husks (35–40 small husks), soaked in water to cover overnight, drained, and patted dry

1. To make the filling, in a frying pan over medium-high heat, warm the olive oil. Add the onion and sauté until softened, about 3 minutes. Add the garlic and cook for 1 minute longer. Add the oregano and green chiles and mix well. Season with salt and set aside.

2. To make the *masa,* in a bowl, stir together the blue cornmeal, yellow cornmeal, baking powder, and salt. Place the lard or shortening in an electric mixer fitted with the paddle attachment and beat on low speed while adding the dry ingredients by the spoonful. Slowly add the stock until well blended, then beat on high until light and fluffy, about 12 minutes.

3. Using 2 or 3 corn husks, tear 18 lengthwise strips, each about ⅛ inch (3 mm) wide, and set aside. Lay out a row of husks on a flat work surface. Place 2 tablespoons of the *masa* in the center of each and spread into a 2-by-3-inch (5-by-7.5-cm) rectangle. Place about 1 tablespoon filling in the center. Bring the sides of the corn husk together, which will cause the *masa* to enclose the filling, and wrap the husk around the *masa.* Fold up the ends of the husk and tie in place by running a husk strip lengthwise around the tamale. Repeat until all the tamales are wrapped.

4. Pour water to a depth of 2–3 inches (5–7.5 cm) into the bottom of a steamer. Place the steamer insert in the steamer and line it with some of the remaining corn husks. Stand the tamales upright in the insert in a single layer. Cover with a few more husks. Cover the steamer, bring the water to a boil, and cook the tamales until firm to the touch, 45–50 minutes. To test, peel away the husk on a tamale; it should separate easily from the *masa.*

5. Let the tamales rest for 5 minutes, then serve.

MAKES ABOUT 18 TAMALES; SERVES 6

NUTRITIONAL ANALYSIS PER SERVING
Calories 505 (Kilojoules 2,121); Protein 6 g; Carbohydrates 44 g; Total Fat 34 g; Saturated Fat 12 g; Cholesterol 27 mg; Sodium 542 mg; Dietary Fiber 4 g

The word *tamale* derives from *tamalli,* Nahuatl for "wrapped food." In general, it describes a carefully assembled rectangular packet. At the center is a filling of beef, pork, or chicken in red or green chile sauce, or sometimes simply beans or cheese or vegetables. A layer of *masa* (cornmeal dough) traps the filling, and the whole thing is wrapped in a corn husk and steamed.

Long before the Spanish arrived, the indigenous peoples of Central and South America were eating tamales daily and using them as offerings in sacred rituals, a practice reflected in the presence of tamales at contemporary celebrations for the Day of the Dead and Christmas Eve. Early Southwesterners were quick to adopt the versatile tamale, and today it appears in countless variations on tables throughout the region.

Each state, with the exception of Colorado, claims a tamale specialty, however. In New Mexico, the ubiquitous packets traditionally conceal shredded pork in pure red chile sauce. Fresh corn tamales rule in Arizona and are often unstuffed or laced with a strip of green chile, and held together with just a small amount of *masa.* Texas, not surprisingly, is home

Tamales

to a tamale loaded with beef in cumin-scented red chile sauce.

Well-known restaurant chefs in the area such as Mark Miller in Santa Fe have created menus of cutting-edge tamales to serve alongside the traditional ones. Among his creative offerings are sweet blackberry blue corn tamales and fresh corn tamales with white truffles.

Garden Gazpacho

1¼ lb (625 g) ripe tomatoes

½ English (hothouse) cucumber, cut into large chunks

4 large red bell peppers (capsicums) (about 1½ lb/750 g total weight), roasted, peeled, and seeded *(page 138)*

½ yellow bell pepper (capsicum), seeded and cut into ¼-inch (6-mm) dice

2 serrano chiles, minced

1 small red (Spanish) onion, finely chopped

1 clove garlic, minced

2 tablespoons extra-virgin olive oil, plus extra for drizzling

1 tablespoon sherry vinegar

1 teaspoon kosher salt

1 ripe Haas avocado, pitted, peeled, and cut into ¼-inch (6-mm) cubes

1 tablespoon snipped fresh chives

½ teaspoon dried Mexican oregano

Some of the earliest versions of gazpacho, dating back to medieval Spain, were nothing more than cold soups of bread, olive oil, vinegar, garlic, and water. Vegetables, most notably sun-ripened tomatoes, gradually entered the mixture. In my favorite version, garden produce has completely elbowed out the bread, and minced serrano chiles brand the gazpacho with a hint of Southwestern fire.

1. Cut the tomatoes in half crosswise. Using the largest holes on a box grater placed over a bowl, grate the tomato halves. Discard the skins.

2. In a food processor, pulse the cucumber chunks until coarsely puréed. Add to the tomatoes. Place the red bell peppers in the processor and process until the peppers are coarsely puréed. Add to the tomatoes and cucumber.

3. Stir in the yellow bell pepper, chiles, onion, garlic, 2 tablespoons olive oil, vinegar, and salt. Taste and adjust the seasoning. Cover and refrigerate until slightly chilled.

4. Ladle into bowls and garnish with the avocado. Sprinkle with the chives and oregano, then drizzle with a little olive oil. Serve immediately.

SERVES 4

NUTRITIONAL ANALYSIS PER SERVING
Calories 230 (Kilojoules 966); Protein 5 g; Carbohydrates 24 g; Total Fat 15 g; Saturated Fat 2 g; Cholesterol 0 mg; Sodium 392 mg; Dietary Fiber 6 g

Tomatoes and Avocado with Chile Vinaigrette

VINAIGRETTE

2 small cloves garlic, unpeeled

3 large poblano chiles, roasted, peeled, and seeded *(page 138)*

1 tablespoon cider vinegar

pinch of sugar

kosher salt and freshly ground pepper to taste

¾–1 cup (6–8 fl oz/180–250 ml) olive oil

3 lb (1.5 kg) ripe tomatoes *(see note)*

2 ripe Haas avocados, pitted, peeled, and sliced lengthwise

2 tablespoons snipped fresh chives

12 large fresh opal basil or other basil leaves, finely shredded

Small-scale farmers in the Southwest, as elsewhere, are rediscovering the pleasures offered by so-called heirloom tomatoes, old-fashioned varieties that long ago fell out of favor with the growth of large commercial farm operations. From July through September, farmers' markets stock these colorful, flavorful tomatoes, which are showcased in this simple, elegant salad.

1. To make the vinaigrette, in a small, dry frying pan over medium heat, toast the garlic cloves, turning as necessary, until golden, about 8 minutes. Let cool and peel. In a blender, combine the garlic, chiles, vinegar, sugar, salt, and pepper and purée until smooth. If the ingredients do not purée easily, add a little water, 1 tablespoon at a time, to ease the blending. With the motor running, slowly add as much of the oil as needed to emulsify the mixture. It should be the consistency of heavy (double) cream. If the mixture is too thick, add a little water. Taste and adjust the seasoning.

2. Depending on their size and shape, core and slice, halve, or quarter the tomatoes. Arrange the tomatoes and avocado slices on individual salad plates and drizzle each serving with the vinaigrette, dividing evenly. Sprinkle with the chives and the basil and serve immediately.

SERVES 6

NUTRITIONAL ANALYSIS PER SERVING
Calories 461 (Kilojoules 1,936); Protein 4 g; Carbohydrates 21 g; Total Fat 43 g; Saturated Fat 6 g; Cholesterol 0 mg; Sodium 31 mg; Dietary Fiber 5 g

Achiote Shrimp Tostadas

MARINADE

2 tablespoons roasted garlic *(page 92)*

1 package (3½ oz/105 g) *achiote paste, crumbled*

¼ cup (2 fl oz/60 ml) thawed frozen orange juice concentrate

⅓ cup (3 fl oz/80 ml) fresh grapefruit juice

¼ cup (2 fl oz/60 ml) water

2 tablespoons cider vinegar

1 teaspoon cumin seed, toasted and ground *(page 141)*

1 teaspoon freshly ground canela or ½ teaspoon ground cinnamon

pinch of ground allspice or cloves

pinch of kosher salt, or to taste

24 shrimp (prawns), peeled and deveined

MAYONNAISE

1 can (7½ oz/235 g) chipotle chiles in adobo sauce

3 tablespoons roasted garlic *(page 92)*

1 whole egg plus 1 egg yolk

1 tablespoon balsamic vinegar

¾ cup (6 fl oz/180 ml) safflower oil

kosher salt to taste

12 white corn tortillas, each 5 inches (13 cm) in diameter

safflower oil for frying

⅓ cup (½ oz/15 g) snipped fresh chives or coarsely chopped fresh cilantro (fresh coriander)

This appetizer gets its distinctive flavor from two traditional Mexican ingredients, *achiote* paste and chipotle chiles, and a contemporary addition, balsamic vinegar.

1. To make the marinade, in a food processor, combine the garlic, *achiote,* orange juice concentrate, grapefruit juice, water, vinegar, cumin, canela or cinnamon, allspice or cloves, and salt. Purée until smooth.

2. In a bowl, combine the shrimp and ½ cup (4 fl oz/125 ml) of the marinade. Mix well, cover, and set aside at room temperature for 1 hour.

3. To make the mayonnaise, place the chipotle chiles in a blender and purée until smooth. Pass through a fine-mesh sieve. In the food processor, combine ¼ cup (2 fl oz/60 ml) of the purée, the garlic, the whole egg and egg yolk, and the vinegar. Process to blend. Then, with the motor running, slowly add the oil to form a smooth purée. It should be a little thicker than heavy (double) cream. Season with salt. Cover and refrigerate until serving.

4. Using a 2-inch (5-cm) round cookie cutter, cut out 2 rounds from each tortilla. Pour safflower oil to a depth of ¼ inch (6 mm) into a frying pan and heat over medium-high heat. When the oil is hot, add the tortilla rounds, in batches, and fry until crisp, 1–1½ minutes. Using tongs, transfer to paper towels to drain. Pour off all the oil from the pan.

5. Drain the shrimp well. In the frying pan over medium-high heat, warm 2 tablespoons safflower oil. Add half of the shrimp and cook, turning once, until opaque throughout, 4–6 minutes total. Transfer to a plate. Repeat with the remaining shrimp, adding oil as necessary.

6. Place 1 shrimp on each tortilla round and drizzle with ½ teaspoon of the mayonnaise. (Reserve the remaining mayonnaise for another use.) Sprinkle with chives or cilantro and serve immediately.

SERVES 6

NUTRITIONAL ANALYSIS PER SERVING
Calories 680 (Kilojoules 2,856); Protein 14 g; Carbohydrates 53 g; Total Fat 47 g; Saturated Fat 5 g; Cholesterol 132 mg; Sodium 799 mg; Dietary Fiber 4 g

Southwest
Chiles

Chiles have been cultivated in the Southwest for at least a millennium, and today New Mexico is the nation's largest producer of the heat-packed pods. They are an integral ingredient in countless regional dishes, from chiles rellenos to green chile stew to chili con carne to a legion of salsas.

A bewildering number of distinct chile species and varieties exist, all with different heat levels and flavors and in different shapes, sizes, and shades. Correctly identifying them is complicated by the fact that a green chile and a red, orange, or yellow chile may simply be different stages of ripeness of the same pepper. Green signals the unripened stage, while the other colors characterize a ripened, or mature, chile. To add to the confusion, the same chile can also have different names, depending on whether it is fresh or dried and sometimes where it is grown.

A bounty of chiles is displayed in markets throughout the Southwest, and discriminating shoppers are regularly seen carefully picking through bins of poblanos and serranos, moritas and chipotles. They are looking for smooth, shiny, firm fresh pods that are heavy for their size, and for clean, evenly colored dried chiles with no breaks.

Southwest cooks are blessed with a wealth of chiles. Here are a handful of the most commonly used.

Ancho Dried form of the poblano chile, broad shouldered, wrinkled, and filled with sweet heat. Also commonly ground.

Chile Caribe Finely crushed dried New Mexico red chiles.

Chipotle Dried, smoked version of a jalapeño varietal. Also available canned *en adobo,* in a spicy tomato-vinegar sauce.

Guajillo Slender, earthy, deep red dried chile, about 6 inches (15 cm) long and with a tannic heat.

Jalapeño Popular thick-fleshed fresh green or red chiles that carry high heat. Also available pickled, labeled *en escabeche.*

Morita Deep red, wrinkly skinned dried chile with smoky high heat.

New Mexico Green Fresh green chile, 5 to 9 inches (13 to 23 cm) long, varying in strength between mild and medium-hot.

New Mexico Red Dark red mature form of the New Mexico green, used fresh and dried. Those grown in the Chimayó region of New Mexico, often labeled simply as **Chimayó** chiles, are known for their intense flavor. Available dried whole or ground.

Poblano Medium-sized, cone-shaped fresh chile, available both dark green and dark red-brown, mild to pleasantly hot.

Serrano Small, slim green or red fresh chiles with bright, clean searing heat.

A sampling of fresh and dried chiles of the Southwest (clockwise from left): habaneros, chilacas, serranos, güeros, and red jalapeños (opposite); and guajillo, pequin, ancho, de Arbol, and cascabel (below).

Sopa de Lima

1 lb (500 g) skinless, boneless chicken breasts

1 large, ripe Haas avocado

6 cups (48 fl oz/1.5 l) chicken stock

¼ cup (2 fl oz/60 ml) fresh lime juice, plus 6 lime wedges

kosher salt to taste

¾ cup (4½ oz/140 g) diced ripe plum (Roma) tomato

6 tablespoons (2 oz/60 g) finely chopped red (Spanish) onion

3 serrano chiles, minced

3 tablespoons coarsely chopped fresh cilantro (fresh coriander)

You'll find small, spherical, yellow-green limes, the *limas* of southern Mexico, in ethnic markets in the Southwest. The fruit has a flavor reminiscent of bergamot, the citrus fruit whose oil scents Earl Grey tea, and it contributes a light, refreshing quality to this chicken-and-vegetable soup. Similar Key limes make a good substitute, although you can also use common Persian limes.

1. In a medium saucepan, combine the chicken with water to cover by 3 inches (7.5 cm). Bring to a boil over high heat, reduce the heat to medium-low, and simmer the chicken gently until opaque throughout, about 10 minutes. Remove from the heat and let the chicken cool in the liquid. Lift out the chicken and discard the water. Using your fingers, shred the chicken into strips.

2. Halve and pit the avocado, then peel. Cut each half in half again lengthwise, then cut crosswise into ½-inch (12-mm) cubes.

3. In a saucepan, bring the stock to a boil. Season with the lime juice and salt. Divide the chicken, avocado, tomato, onion, chiles, and cilantro evenly among individual bowls. Ladle the hot stock over the top, again dividing evenly. Serve immediately, accompanying each bowl with a lime wedge for diners to add more juice to taste.

SERVES 6

NUTRITIONAL ANALYSIS PER SERVING
Calories 195 (Kilojoules 819); Protein 21 g; Carbohydrates 8 g; Total Fat 9 g; Saturated Fat 2 g; Cholesterol 44 mg; Sodium 1,057 mg; Dietary Fiber 1 g

Smoked Trout with Purslane and Honeydew

DRESSING

3 tablespoons fresh lemon juice

1 tablespoon honey

grated zest of 1 lemon

3 tablespoons lemon-flavored olive oil

3 tablespoons safflower oil

kosher salt and freshly ground white
   pepper to taste

1 lb (500 g) young purslane, trimmed
   into small sprigs

2 cups (4 oz/125 g) mixed salad
   greens

1 lb (500 g) smoked trout fillets,
   skinned

1 small, ripe honeydew melon, halved,
   seeded, peeled, and cut into small
   cubes

6 green (spring) onions, including
   tender green tops, sliced on the
   extreme diagonal

2 tablespoons coarsely chopped
   fresh mint

2 tablespoons coarsely chopped fresh
   cilantro (fresh coriander)

Trout is widely farmed in New Mexico, Arizona, and Colorado, and is also found wild in the rivers and streams of the same states. Succulent, slightly tart purslane grows unchecked in the spring and summer all over New Mexico, where it is called *verdolagas*. Look in farmers' markets for small, crisp, tender leaves. In their absence, substitute watercress.

1. To make the dressing, in a bowl, whisk together the lemon juice, honey, lemon zest, and olive and safflower oils. Season with salt and white pepper and set aside.

2. In a bowl, combine the purslane and greens and toss gently. Divide the greens among individual salad plates.

3. Break the trout fillets into 1-inch (2.5-cm) pieces, removing any errant bones, and place in a bowl. Add the honeydew, green onions, mint, and cilantro. Drizzle with 6 tablespoons (3 fl oz/90 ml) of the dressing and toss to coat evenly. Arrange a portion of the trout mixture in the center of each serving of greens. Drizzle the greens with the remaining dressing. Serve immediately.

SERVES 6

NUTRITIONAL ANALYSIS PER SERVING
Calories 359 (Kilojoules 1,508); Protein 21 g; Carbohydrates 23 g; Total Fat 22 g;
Saturated Fat 4 g; Cholesterol 20 mg; Sodium 843 mg; Dietary Fiber 2 g

Red Snapper Ceviche

⅓ cup (3 fl oz/80 ml) fresh orange juice

¼ cup (2 fl oz/60 ml) fresh lemon juice

3 tablespoons fresh lime juice

pinch of kosher salt

pinch of sugar, or to taste

½ lb (250 g) red snapper fillet

12 cherry tomatoes, stems removed and quartered

1 small, ripe Haas avocado, pitted, peeled, and cubed

½ small red (Spanish) onion, slivered

½ cup (2½ oz/75 g) cubed English (hothouse) cucumber

1 or 2 serrano chiles, minced

1 tablespoon chopped fresh mint

2 tablespoons chopped fresh cilantro (fresh coriander)

2 tablespoons lemon- or lime-flavored olive oil

4 fresh mint or cilantro (fresh coriander) sprigs

The popular Mexican technique for "cooking" fresh raw seafood by tossing it with citrus juice finds favor in many restaurants and homes in the Southwest. This version adds a generous amount of vegetables and herbs to the traditional mixture. Choose only the freshest red snapper.

1. In a nonaluminum bowl, stir together the orange, lemon, and lime juices. Season with salt and enough sugar to balance the acid of the citrus juices.

2. Check the fish fillet for errant bones, then cut into ½-inch (12-mm) cubes. Add to the citrus juice mixture, immersing the fish completely. Cover and refrigerate for 1 hour.

3. In a bowl, combine the tomatoes, avocado, onion, cucumber, chiles to taste, mint, and cilantro and stir gently to combine.

4. Transfer the fish to a colander and let drain for several seconds, then add the fish to the tomato mixture and mix gently. Drizzle with the oil and taste and adjust the seasoning with salt.

5. Divide the ceviche among martini glasses or small glass bowls and garnish with the mint or cilantro sprigs. Serve at once.

SERVES 4

NUTRITIONAL ANALYSIS PER SERVING
Calories 195 (Kilojoules 819); Protein 13 g; Carbohydrates 7 g; Total Fat 13 g; Saturated Fat 2 g; Cholesterol 21 mg; Sodium 55 mg; Dietary Fiber 2 g

Beets with Ruby Grapefruit and Pomegranate

The Southwesterner's appreciation for sweet, tart, and earthy flavors finds memorable expression in a salad whose vivid colors remind me of an Arizona sunset. Pomegranates are in season only briefly in late fall and early winter, so act quickly when you see them in the market.

8 beets, about 2 lb (1 kg) total weight

kosher salt to taste

2–3 tablespoons olive oil

1 large and 1 small pomegranate

sugar to taste

6 tablespoons (3 fl oz/90 ml) orange-flavored olive oil

2 large Ruby grapefruits

2 bunches watercress, tough stems removed

1. If the beet greens are intact, trim them off, leaving 1 inch (2.5 cm) of the stems. Place the unpeeled beets in a saucepan with water to cover by 3 inches (7.5 cm). Bring to a boil over high heat, add salt, cover partially, reduce the heat to medium, and simmer until tender, about 40 minutes. Drain and let cool slightly, then peel and cut each beet into 6 wedges. Place in a bowl, add the 2–3 tablespoons olive oil and toss to coat lightly. Sprinkle with salt and set aside.

2. Cut an X at the flower end of the large pomegranate and split it open into quarters. Holding each quarter over a bowl, and using a fingertip, loosen the seeds so they drop into the bowl. Place the seeds in a medium-mesh sieve over a small nonaluminum bowl and press with the back of a wooden spoon to express the juice. You should have ⅓–½ cup (3–4 fl oz/80–125 ml) juice. Repeat with the small pomegranate, but do not express the juice. Add sugar and salt to the juice and whisk in the orange-flavored oil. Taste and adjust the seasoning. Set aside.

3. Working with 1 grapefruit at a time, cut a slice off the top and bottom to expose the flesh. Stand the fruit upright and thickly cut off the peel in strips to expose the flesh. Holding the fruit over a bowl, cut along either side of each section, letting it drop into the bowl.

4. Arrange the watercress sprigs, grapefruit sections, and beets on individual plates. Drizzle each salad with about 2 tablespoons of the dressing, sprinkle with the pomegranate seeds, and serve.

SERVES 6

NUTRITIONAL ANALYSIS PER SERVING
Calories 274 (Kilojoules 1,151); Protein 4 g; Carbohydrates 35 g; Total Fat 19 g; Saturated Fat 3 g; Cholesterol 0 mg; Sodium 98 mg; Dietary Fiber 3 g

Farmers' Market Roasted Tomato Soup

2 lb (1 kg) ripe tomatoes, halved and seeded

3 poblano chiles, roasted, peeled, and seeded (*page 138*)

3 small fennel bulbs, stems and feathery tops trimmed and bulbs cut lengthwise into 8 wedges

2 large leeks, white and pale green parts only, halved lengthwise and cut into 1-inch (2.5-cm) chunks

6 shallots, quartered lengthwise

6 cloves garlic

leaves from 4 large fresh thyme sprigs, chopped

leaves from 1 large fresh rosemary sprig, chopped

¼ cup (2 fl oz/60 ml) extra-virgin olive oil

kosher salt and freshly ground pepper to taste

3 cups (24 fl oz/750 ml) vegetable or chicken stock, or more if needed

½ cup (4 fl oz/125 ml) crema or crème fraîche

2 tablespoons snipped fresh chives

2 tablespoons coarsely chopped fresh flat-leaf (Italian) parsley

On a hot summer's day in Santa Fe or Scottsdale, you could quickly breeze through the local farmers' market and fill your basket with nearly all the ingredients you'll need for this full-bodied, fragrant soup. Serve the soup with cornmeal muffins or sage-scented biscuits.

1. Preheat the oven to 450°F (230°C). Line 2 baking sheets with aluminum foil.

2. In a large bowl, combine the tomatoes, chiles, fennel, leeks, shallots, garlic, thyme, and rosemary. Add the olive oil, salt, and pepper and toss well. Divide the mixture evenly between the prepared baking sheets.

3. Place 1 baking sheet on the top oven rack and the other baking sheet on the bottom rack. Roast until the edges of the vegetables on top are crisp and lightly browned, about 15 minutes. Stir the vegetables, then switch the baking sheets. Continue to roast until all the vegetables are browned but not dried out, 10–12 minutes longer. Remove from the oven and let cool for 10 minutes.

4. In a blender or food processor, process the roasted vegetables and the 3 cups (24 fl oz/750 ml) stock, in batches, until smooth. Pass the purée through a coarse-mesh sieve into a saucepan.

5. Place the saucepan over medium heat and warm to serving temperature, stirring often. If the soup seems too thick, add more stock.

6. Ladle the soup into warmed bowls and garnish each serving with some crema or crème fraîche and a sprinkle of chives and parsley. Serve immediately.

SERVES 6

NUTRITIONAL ANALYSIS PER SERVING
Calories 268 (Kilojoules 1,126); Protein 5 g; Carbohydrates 25 g; Total Fat 18 g; Saturated Fat 6 g; Cholesterol 17 mg; Sodium 643 mg; Dietary Fiber 4 g

2 Seafood, Poultry & Meats

Southwesterners regularly sit down to hearty, well-seasoned main dishes that stretch across the pantry. They like their meat, of course, whether it's beef rolled up in tortillas, steak cooked over coals, or pork doused with tomato salsa or in a green chile stew. Lamb, introduced by the Spanish, is a favorite, too, sometimes simply grilled and served in a stylish salad. Chicken, a mainstay, might be stuffed and roasted for Sunday supper or mixed with green chiles inside enchiladas. Fish farms and mountain rivers supply fresh trout for the table, and the states' chefs have introduced fish tacos and seafood stews to a population that now claims them as regional plates.

Seafood Stew in Smoky Tomato Broth

TOMATO BROTH

3 tablespoons extra-virgin olive oil

1 small white onion, slivered

2 cloves garlic, minced

1 teaspoon dried Mexican oregano

1 bay leaf

1 can (15 oz/470 g) whole tomatoes with juice, puréed

1 can (15 oz/470 g) diced tomatoes with juice

3 chipotle chiles in adobo sauce, finely chopped

pinch of sugar

kosher salt and freshly ground pepper

STEW

3 tablespoons olive oil

2 cloves garlic, minced

18 extra-large shrimp (prawns), peeled and deveined

18 small mussels, well scrubbed and debearded

18 small hard-shell clams, well scrubbed

3 cups (24 fl oz/750 ml) bottled clam juice

1½ cups (12 fl oz/375 ml) water

kosher salt to taste

2 cups (10 oz/315 g) Seasoned White Rice (*page 94*)

2 tablespoons coarsely chopped fresh cilantro (fresh coriander), plus sprigs for garnish

1 lime, cut into 6 wedges

This recipe owes its existence to my favorite fish purveyor in Santa Fe, Above Sea Level, who consistently provides me with good fresh seafood. It resembles a traditional Mexican *sopa de mariscos* (shellfish stew), with the added flourish of a smoky tomato broth that adds a north-of-the-border influence.

1. To make the tomato broth, in a large saucepan over medium-high heat, warm the olive oil. Add the onion and sauté until translucent, about 3 minutes. Add the garlic, oregano, and bay leaf and sauté for 1 minute. Add the puréed and diced tomatoes and juice and the chipotles and season to taste with sugar, salt, and pepper. Simmer, uncovered, until slightly thickened, about 20 minutes. Set aside.

2. To make the stew, in a large, deep frying pan over medium-high heat, warm the olive oil. Add the garlic and sauté for 1 minute. Add the shrimp and sauté until they just turn pink and are opaque throughout, 2–3 minutes. Remove the shrimp from the pan and keep warm. Add the mussels and clams, discarding any that fail to close to the touch. Pour in the tomato broth, bottled clam juice, and water and season with salt. Cover and simmer until the mussels and clams open, 3–4 minutes. Uncover and discard any shellfish that failed to open.

3. Place a scoop of rice in the center of each of 6 large, wide-rimmed soup plates. Arrange 3 shrimp, 3 mussels, and 3 clams around the rice. Stir the chopped cilantro into the remaining broth. Taste and adjust the seasoning. Ladle enough of the broth into each of the soup plates to fill just below the rim. Garnish each serving with a cilantro sprig along with a wedge of lime, to be squeezed onto the stew before eating. Serve at once.

SERVES 6

NUTRITIONAL ANALYSIS PER SERVING
Calories 373 (Kilojoules 1,567); Protein 30 g; Carbohydrates 26 g; Total Fat 17 g; Saturated Fat 2 g; Cholesterol 161 mg; Sodium 641 mg; Dietary Fiber 2 g

Capon with Chorizo–Corn Bread Stuffing

CORN BREAD

1 cup (5 oz/155 g) each unbleached all-purpose (plain) flour and stone-ground yellow cornmeal

2 tablespoons sugar

2 teaspoons baking powder

pinch of kosher salt

1¼ cups (10 fl oz/310 ml) buttermilk

1 egg, lightly beaten

¼ cup (2 oz/60 g) unsalted butter, melted

STUFFING

3–4 tablespoons olive oil

1 white onion, finely diced

1 carrot, peeled and finely diced

1 celery stalk, finely diced

1 clove garlic, minced

1½ lb (750 g) chorizo, casings removed

1 cup (6 oz/185 g) roasted, peeled, seeded, and chopped New Mexico green chile (*page 138*)

1 cup (3 oz/90 g) dried apples, chopped

1 tablespoon each chopped fresh sage and marjoram

1–2 cups (8–16 fl oz/250–500 ml) chicken stock

3 tablespoons unsalted butter, melted

kosher salt and freshly ground pepper to taste

1 capon, 7–8 lb (3.5–4 kg)

2 tablespoons olive oil

kosher salt and freshly ground pepper

1. The day before serving the capon, make the corn bread: Preheat the oven to 350°F (180°C). Butter an 8-inch (20-cm) square pan. In a bowl, stir together the flour, cornmeal, sugar, baking powder, and salt. In another bowl, stir together the buttermilk, egg, and melted butter. Pour the buttermilk mixture into the flour mixture and stir until just combined. Pour into the prepared pan. Bake until golden, about 20 minutes. Transfer to a rack and let cool in the pan, then leave for 1 day to dry out.

2. To make the stuffing, in a frying pan over medium heat, warm the oil. Add the onion, carrot, and celery and sauté until softened, about 8 minutes. Add the garlic and sauté for 1 minute. Transfer to a bowl. Return the frying pan to medium heat. Crumble in the chorizo and fry until cooked through, about 8 minutes. Transfer to a sieve to drain, then add to the vegetables. Stir in the chile, dried apples, sage, and marjoram. Crumble in the corn bread, then add the stock little by little, tossing to incorporate and using only enough to make the mixture damp. Drizzle with the butter. Season with salt and pepper.

3. Preheat the oven to 400°F (200°C). Rinse the capon and pat dry. Fill the cavity loosely with stuffing, then truss closed. Brush the bird with the oil and sprinkle with salt and pepper. Butter a 2½-qt (2.5-l) baking dish and spoon the remaining stuffing into it. Cover with aluminum foil. Place the capon in a roasting pan and roast for 20 minutes. Reduce the temperature to 350°F (180°C) and continue to roast until an instant-read thermometer inserted into the thigh away from the bone registers 170°F (77°C) or the juices run clear when the thigh joint is pierced, about 1¼ hours. The last 30 minutes of roasting, place the baking dish in the oven and bake for 20 minutes. Uncover and continue to bake for 10 minutes.

4. Place the capon on a platter and let rest for 10 minutes. Carve the bird and serve with the stuffing in a dish alongside.

SERVES 6

NUTRITIONAL ANALYSIS PER SERVING
Calories 1,641 (Kilojoules 6,892); Protein 115 g; Carbohydrates 62 g; Total Fat 101 g; Saturated Fat 36 g; Cholesterol 407 mg; Sodium 2,065 mg; Dietary Fiber 3 g

Herbed Chicken Breasts

6 skinless, boneless chicken breast halves

kosher salt and freshly ground black pepper to taste

1½ cups (12 fl oz/375 ml) buttermilk

2½ cups (5 oz/155 g) fresh bread crumbs, made from coarse country bread

2 cloves garlic, minced

leaves from 2 fresh thyme sprigs, chopped

1 teaspoon dried Mexican oregano

1 tablespoon chile caribe or 2 teaspoons red pepper flakes

¾ cup (4 oz/125 ml) all-purpose (plain) flour

2 eggs

2 tablespoons heavy (double) cream

6 tablespoons (3 fl oz/90 ml) olive oil

Marinating the thinly pounded breasts in buttermilk and then coating them with fresh bread crumbs and lively seasonings produces an especially elegant and flavorful fried chicken. This dish is wonderful hot or cold, with mashed potatoes or Texas Potato Salad (page 102) and Tart and Tangy Coleslaw (page 104).

1. One at a time, place the chicken breasts between 2 sheets of plastic wrap and, using a meat pounder, pound to an even ¼-inch (6-mm) thickness. Season the breasts with salt and black pepper and place them in a lock-top plastic bag. Pour in the buttermilk and seal closed. Place in the refrigerator for at least 1 hour or up to overnight.

2. In a food processor, combine the bread crumbs, garlic, thyme, oregano, chile caribe or red pepper flakes, and a pinch of salt. Pulse a few times to mix the ingredients thoroughly. Transfer to a shallow pan.

3. Spread the flour on a flat plate. In a shallow bowl, lightly beat the eggs with the cream. Remove the chicken from the buttermilk and pat dry with paper towels. Working with 1 breast half at a time, coat both sides with flour, shaking to remove the excess. Then dip it in the egg mixture and finally coat it with the seasoned crumbs, pressing the crumbs lightly to adhere. Place on a rack. Repeat with the remaining chicken.

4. Line a baking sheet with aluminum foil. In a nonstick frying pan over medium-high heat, warm the olive oil. Add 2 chicken breast halves to the pan and cook, turning once, until golden on the outside and opaque throughout, about 3 minutes on each side. Transfer to the prepared baking sheet and keep warm in a low oven while cooking the remaining chicken.

5. Transfer the chicken breasts to warmed individual plates and serve.

SERVES 6

NUTRITIONAL ANALYSIS PER SERVING
Calories 434 (Kilojoules 1,823); Protein 34 g; Carbohydrates 28 g; Total Fat 20 g; Saturated Fat 4 g; Cholesterol 147 mg; Sodium 228 mg; Dietary Fiber 1 g

Outsiders can't resist ribbing Southwesterners about the local wines. Indeed, how many times have residents been asked, "Is it made of cactus juice or snake venom?" But such wags are quickly silenced once they sip a glass of a very respectable Southwest Zinfandel or Chardonnay.

Making wine in this part of the country is a challenge, however. Extremes of weather, altitude, terrain, and soil demand special attention. At the same time, a number of natural advantages exist. The phylloxera louse, a formidable enemy of the wine grape, cannot thrive in the arid climate, nor can most rot, mold, or mildew fungi. During the winter, cold temperatures at high altitudes mean few insects and other pests, making organic or reduced-pesticide vineyards possible.

These inherent benefits undoubtedly helped the Franciscan priests who planted the New World's first wine grapes in New Mexico in 1662. At about the same time, Spanish missionaries began cultivation in Texas. Arizona's wine industry was launched in the nineteenth century, as was Colorado's. Prohibition halted these efforts, however, and it wasn't until

Southwest **Wines**

the late 1960s that the Southwest resurrected its wine industry.

Today, there are about eighty wineries throughout the region, and that number is continuing to grow. Locally bottled Sauvignon Blancs, Cabernets, and Merlots regularly turn up on local dinner tables. It may be only a boomlet, but once-skeptical wine lovers are now taking notice.

Skirt Steak Fajitas with Avocado Salsa

MARINADE

4 small navel or other seedless oranges, peeled, halved, and each half quartered

½ can (7 oz/220 g can) chipotle chiles in adobo sauce

1 white onion, halved and each half quartered

3 large cloves garlic

leaves from 4 fresh rosemary springs

leaves from 3 fresh marjoram sprigs

1 bunch fresh cilantro (fresh coriander), cut crosswise into thirds

1 teaspoon kosher salt

freshly ground pepper to taste

2 lb (1 kg) skirt steak, trimmed of surface fat and silver skin and cut in half horizontally

SALSA

3 ripe Haas avocados, pitted

1 red (Spanish) onion, diced

2 cloves garlic, minced

¼ cup (⅓ oz/10 g) coarsely chopped fresh cilantro (fresh coriander)

2–3 tablespoons fresh lime juice, or to taste

kosher salt to taste

2 limes, quartered

kosher salt and freshly ground pepper to taste

12 flour tortillas, heated

The orange flavor and smoky heat of the marinade give this skirt steak unforgettable character. Carved into strips after grilling, the meat is served with salsa atop warm flour tortillas for wrapping up, burrito style.

1. To make the marinade, in a food processor, combine the oranges, chipotle chiles, onion, garlic, rosemary, marjoram, and cilantro. Process until the ingredients are thoroughly combined, resulting in a coarse purée. Season with salt and pepper.

2. Pour a thin layer of the marinade into a baking dish, add the steak, and top evenly with the remaining marinade. Cover and refrigerate for 6 hours or up to overnight.

3. To make the salsa, cut the avocado halves in half again lengthwise, and then make short horizontal cuts through the flesh of each quarter to create large chunks. Using a spoon, scoop the chunks from the skin into a bowl. Add the onion, garlic, cilantro, lime juice, and salt and stir to combine. Taste and adjust the seasoning. Cover with plastic wrap, pressing it directly onto the surface of the salsa, and set aside.

4. Prepare a fire in a charcoal grill.

5. Remove the meat from the refrigerator 30 minutes before grilling and scrape off the marinade. Squeeze the juice from the limes over the meat and sprinkle with salt and pepper.

6. Place the meat on the grill rack about 4 inches (10 cm) from the coals and grill, turning once, for about 3 minutes on each side. Transfer to a cutting board, let rest for 5 minutes, and then slice into thin strips.

7. Top each warmed tortilla with some of the sliced steak and divide among warmed plates. Serve with the salsa.

SERVES 6

NUTRITIONAL ANALYSIS PER SERVING
Calories 682 (Kilojoules 2,864); Protein 38 g; Carbohydrates 57 g; Total Fat 35 g; Saturated Fat 9 g; Cholesterol 75 mg; Sodium 570 mg; Dietary Fiber 6 g

Texas Baby Back Ribs

SAUCE

¾ cup (6 fl oz/180 ml) white wine vinegar

¾ cup (6 fl oz/180 ml) cider vinegar

⅓ cup (3 fl oz/80 ml) Worcestershire sauce

1 tablespoon dried Mexican oregano

2 teaspoons paprika

1 teaspoon each garlic salt, garlic powder, onion salt, and onion powder

1 teaspoon each coriander and cumin seed, toasted and ground (page 141)

1 teaspoon freshly ground canela or ½ teaspoon ground cinnamon

1 teaspoon dry mustard

½ teaspoon ground allspice

10 shakes liquid smoke

2 tablespoons chipotle seasoning or 1 tablespoon puréed chipotle chiles in adobo sauce

2 tablespoons ground Chimayó chile

½ cup (4 fl oz/125 ml) chili sauce

½ cup (3½ oz/105 g) firmly packed dark brown sugar

¼ cup (2 fl oz/60 ml) tamarind concentrate

¼ cup (3 oz/90 g) honey

3 sides baby back ribs, 4½–5½ lb (2.25–2.75 kg) total weight

3 tablespoons rendered bacon fat

Even though Texas is beef country, I like the way that the state's favored spicy, vinegary, not-too-sweet barbecue sauce goes with the rich, sweet flavor of pork. If you like, though, try this sauce with meaty beef ribs or steaks.

1. To make the sauce, in a bowl, combine the wine vinegar, cider vinegar, Worcestershire sauce, oregano, paprika, garlic salt and powder, onion salt and powder, coriander, cumin, canela or cinnamon, dry mustard, allspice, liquid smoke, chipotle seasoning or chipotle purée, ground chile, chili sauce, brown sugar, tamarind concentrate, and honey. Mix well. Pour half of the mixture into the bottom of a large baking dish. Trim the membrane from the nonmeaty side of the rib slabs and place the ribs on top of the sauce. Turn them to coat on both sides. Pour the remaining sauce over the ribs, cover, and refrigerate overnight.

2. Preheat the oven to 350°F (180°C). Line a 14-by-18-inch (35-by-45-cm) baking sheet with 1-inch (2.5-cm) sides with aluminum foil. Place a large wire rack on the baking sheet.

3. Remove the ribs from the sauce, reserving the sauce. Place the ribs, meaty side up, on the rack. Bake, basting with ¼ cup (2 fl oz/60 ml) sauce, until the ribs are tender, about 1¼ hours.

4. While the ribs are baking, pour the remaining sauce into a saucepan with the bacon fat. Bring to a boil, reduce the heat to medium, and simmer, uncovered, until thickened, 25–30 minutes. Keep warm.

5. Serve each diner half a rack of ribs. To cut the ribs for each serving, hold the half rack with tongs and cut between the bones with a large sharp knife. Serve the reheated sauce on the side.

SERVES 6

NUTRITIONAL ANALYSIS PER SERVING
Calories 904 (Kilojoules 3,797); Protein 46 g; Carbohydrates 46 g; Total Fat 60 g; Saturated Fat 22 g; Cholesterol 220 mg; Sodium 1,320 mg; Dietary Fiber 1 g

Outdoor
Cooking

The Southwesterners of today are consummate outdoor cooks. They follow in the tradition of the Pueblo Indians and their pit cooking, the Spanish and their hornos, the early traders and miners and their campfires, and the rugged chuck wagon cooks who fueled the robust appetites of hard-working cowboys.

The pit cooking of the Pueblos was simple yet efficient. They dug a hole, lined it with stones, and then set a fire in it. Once the wood was reduced to glowing embers, the Indians wrapped meat in leaves or burlap and placed it in the coals. They covered and sealed the pit, and a dozen hours later, everyone feasted on tender meat.

The Spanish introduced hornos, beehive-shaped outdoor adobe ovens, to the Pueblo Indians, who quickly adopted them for baking their traditional breads. They lit a fire in the oven, and when it had burned down, they placed the shaped dough inside and sealed the oven opening. The bread baked slowly, producing a crisp-crusted loaf with a good crumb.

The dutch oven arrived with the nineteenth-century fur traders, miners, and early settlers. Originally designed by manufacturers in Holland for baking foods over an open fire, the unique iron pot stood on stubby legs over a campfire, while its rimmed lid held additional coals for even cooking. A modernized dutch oven continues to hold an important place in the Southwest kitchen.

The chuck wagon cook relied on the dutch oven as well. The wagon itself was a no-frills traveling kitchen outfitted with equipment and supplies to feed hungry cowboys out on the range. In addition to a dutch oven, the chuck wagon carried kettles, frying pans, griddles, and a large coffee pot, all of which were used over a campfire. These simple outdoor dinner menus usually included beef stew or beef steak along with beans, hot bread, and pies filled with stewed dried fruits.

Outdoor cooking remains popular in the Southwest. Today, however, cooking over an open fire is called grilling, while barbecuing is the modern version of pit cooking. The smoke that curls around the cooking foods, whether in a specially designed smoker or through a simple grate placed over a fire, is created by the addition of aromatic wood chips,

grapevine prunings, or desert sage to the fire.

The fare has changed along with the equipment. In place of simple beef and beans, contemporary home cooks serve grilled vegetables and fajitas with fresh fruit salsa. Restaurant chefs inevitably offer a variety of foods cooked on a grill or in a barbecue or smoker. Yet despite such innovations, Southwesterners know that the outdoor cooking of today was born in the traditions of yesterday.

A cast-iron pot is an ideal vessel for cooking beans and stews outdoors (opposite). Mesquite charcoal, vine clippings, and hickory smoking chips add flavor to grilled and barbecued foods (below).

Grilled Lamb Salad with Tomato Vinaigrette

1 boneless lamb top (from top of leg),
2 lb (1 kg)

leaves from 4 fresh rosemary sprigs
and 6 fresh thyme sprigs

3 cloves garlic, thinly sliced

kosher salt and freshly ground pepper
to taste

3 tablespoons extra-virgin olive oil

2 leeks, white part only, julienned

2 small red (Spanish) onions, cut into
sixths through the root end

2 small fennel bulbs, trimmed and
cut into sixths through the core

1 yellow bell pepper (capsicum),
seeded and cut into wide strips

olive oil as needed

1 lb (500 g) asparagus, trimmed

¾ lb (375 g) haricots verts, trimmed
and boiled until tender

2 tablespoons coarsely chopped
mixed fresh herbs of choice

VINAIGRETTE

3 ripe plum (Roma) tomatoes

2 serrano chiles

1 small white onion, sliced ½ inch
(12 mm) thick

3 cloves garlic, unpeeled

2 teaspoons chopped fresh mint

1 teaspoon chopped fresh marjoram

fresh lemon juice, sugar, kosher salt,
and freshly ground pepper to taste

½ cup (4 fl oz/125 ml) olive oil

1. Place the lamb in a bowl and toss with the rosemary, thyme, garlic, salt, pepper, and the extra-virgin olive oil. Cover and let stand at room temperature for 2 hours or up to overnight in the refrigerator.

2. To make the vinaigrette, place the tomatoes and chiles in a cast-iron frying pan over medium-high heat and char on all sides. Set aside to cool. Char the onion slices and garlic cloves in the same way and let cool. Peel the tomatoes and place in a food processor. Finely chop the chiles, coarsely chop the onion, and peel and mince the garlic. Add to the processor and process until the tomatoes are coarsely puréed. Pour into a bowl and mix in the mint, marjoram, lemon juice, sugar, salt, and pepper. Stir in the oil. Taste and adjust the seasoning. Set aside.

3. In a bowl, combine the leeks with ice water to cover. Let stand for 1 hour. Drain, cover, and refrigerate until needed. Meanwhile, preheat the oven to 475°F (245°C). Line a baking sheet with aluminum foil. In a bowl, toss together the onions, fennel, and bell pepper with a little olive oil, salt, and pepper. Spread on the prepared baking sheet. Roast until the vegetables are crisp, about 12 minutes. Let cool. Toss the asparagus in a little olive oil, salt, and pepper and roast until just tender, 5–6 minutes. Add to the other vegetables and let cool. Add the haricots verts to the other vegetables, toss, and set aside.

4. Replace the foil on the baking sheet. In a frying pan over medium-high heat, warm 3 tablespoons olive oil. Add the lamb and brown well on all sides, about 7 minutes. Transfer to the prepared baking sheet and roast until medium-rare, 20–25 minutes, or to your taste. Let cool.

5. Slice the lamb against the grain and set aside 5 slices for each serving. Reserve the remaining lamb for other uses. For each serving, toss an equal amount of the vegetables with the lamb and place on a plate. Drizzle with the vinaigrette and sprinkle with the herbs and leeks.

SERVES 6–8

NUTRITIONAL ANALYSIS PER SERVING
Calories 583 (Kilojoules 2,449); Protein 29 g; Carbohydrates 19 g; Total Fat 45 g;
Saturated Fat 10 g; Cholesterol 85 mg; Sodium 137 mg; Dietary Fiber 4 g

Salmon Cakes with Jalapeño Rémoulade

JALAPEÑO RÉMOULADE

1 whole egg plus 1 egg yolk

2 teaspoons Dijon mustard

¾ cup (6 fl oz/180 ml) safflower oil

2 cloves garlic, minced

1 tablespoon capers, rinsed

¼ cup (2 oz/60 g) cornichons, rinsed

6 canned pickled jalapeño strips, plus 1 tablespoon juice from can

¼ cup (¾ oz/20 g) thinly sliced green (spring) onion

¼ cup (⅓ oz/10 g) chopped fresh flat-leaf (Italian) parsley

pinch of kosher salt

SALMON CAKES

2 lb (1 kg) salmon fillets, skinned and cut into chunks

1 large red (Spanish) onion, cut into ¼-inch (6-mm) dice

3 tablespoons chopped fresh tarragon

⅓ cup (2 oz/60 g) diced roasted red bell pepper (capsicum) *(page 138)*

1 cup (2 oz/60 g) fresh bread crumbs

½ teaspoon kosher salt

1 teaspoon white pepper

1 cup (5 oz/155 g) unbleached all-purpose (plain) flour

2 eggs

1 tablespoon water

2 cups (4 oz/125 g) *panko*

½ cup (4 fl oz/125 ml) vegetable oil

Strips of pickled jalapeño chile spike a traditional French-style tartar sauce to give this dish a Southwestern accent.

1. To make the rémoulade, in a food processor, combine the whole egg, egg yolk, and mustard. Pulse to mix. With the motor running, slowly pour in the oil and process until the mixture forms a thick mayonnaise. Add the garlic, capers, cornichons, and jalapeño strips and juice and pulse until finely chopped. Add the green onion and parsley and pulse to mix. Season with salt, transfer to a bowl, cover, and refrigerate.

2. Rinse the processor bowl. To make the salmon cakes, in 2 batches, place the salmon chunks in the processor and pulse until coarsely chopped. Transfer to a bowl. Add the onion, tarragon, bell pepper, and bread crumbs and mix gently. Season with the salt and white pepper.

3. Line a baking sheet with aluminum foil. With a ¼-cup (2-oz/60-g) measure, scoop out the salmon mixture and shape into flat patties about ¾ inch (2 cm) thick. Arrange on the prepared baking sheet and freeze for 20–30 minutes.

4. Line a baking sheet with paper towels. Spread the flour on a flat plate. In a shallow bowl, lightly beat the eggs with the water. Spread the *panko* on a flat plate. In a frying pan over medium-high heat, warm ¼ cup (2 fl oz/60 ml) of the oil. Coat 3 or 4 of the salmon cakes with flour, shaking off any excess. Dip them into the egg, rubbing it into the flour and then into the *panko,* pressing to adhere. Add the cakes to the hot oil and fry, turning once, until golden and cooked through, 2–3 minutes on each side. Transfer to the prepared baking sheet and keep warm in a low oven. Repeat with the remaining cakes, adding the remaining ¼ cup (2 fl oz/60 ml) oil as necessary to prevent sticking.

5. Place 2 salmon cakes on each plate, top with a spoonful or two of rémoulade, and serve.

MAKES 12 CAKES; SERVES 6

NUTRITIONAL ANALYSIS PER CAKE
Calories 475 (Kilojoules 1,993); Protein 20 g; Carbohydrates 22 g; Total Fat 33 g; Saturated Fat 5 g; Cholesterol 116 mg; Sodium 330 mg; Dietary Fiber 1 g

Fish Tacos with Pickled Onions and Chiles

PICKLED ONIONS

1 cup (8 fl oz/250 ml) red wine vinegar

6 tablespoons (3 fl oz/90 ml) thawed frozen orange juice concentrate

⅓ cup (3 oz/90 g) sugar

1½ teaspoons dried Mexican oregano

2 bay leaves (optional)

kosher salt to taste

2 large red (Spanish) onions, thinly sliced

MARINADE

1 large white onion, cut up

2 cloves garlic

3 serrano chiles, stems removed

1 bunch fresh cilantro (fresh coriander), cut into large pieces

1 cup (8 fl oz/250 ml) fresh lime juice

2–3 tablespoons honey

kosher salt to taste

1½ lb (750 g) Chilean sea bass fillet, cut into large cubes

kosher salt and freshly ground pepper to taste

3–4 tablespoons (1½–2 fl oz/ 45–60 ml) olive oil

1½ cups (3 oz/90 g) romaine (cos) lettuce, finely shredded

12 corn tortillas, heated

½ cup (3 oz/90 g) canned pickled jalapeño strips

¾ cup (6 fl oz/180 ml) crema

6 lime wedges

Fish tacos have swept the Southwest in reaction to the growing popularity of fresh seafood. Red snapper or another sea bass can be used in place of the Chilean sea bass, and any leftover pickled onions are good on grilled fish. Serve with fresh salsa.

1. To make the pickled onions, in a bowl, combine the vinegar, orange juice concentrate, sugar, oregano, bay leaves (if using), and salt. Stir until the sugar is dissolved. Add the onions and stir to coat evenly. Cover and let stand at room temperature, stirring occasionally, for 6–8 hours. Refrigerate, covered, until ready to use. The pickled onions will keep for up to 1 month.

2. To make the marinade, in a food processor, combine the onion, garlic, chiles, cilantro, and lime juice. Process until a coarse purée forms. Season to taste with honey and salt. The flavor should be a balance of tart, sweet, salty, and spicy. Pour into a bowl, add the fish, and turn to coat. Cover and marinate at room temperature for 2 hours or refrigerate for up to 4 hours.

3. Remove the fish from the marinade, scraping off the excess marinade, and set aside on paper towels. Sprinkle the fish with salt and pepper.

4. In a large frying pan over medium-high heat, warm the olive oil. Add half of the fish and brown, turning as necessary, until well seared, 1–2 minutes on each side. Transfer the fish to a plate. Repeat with the remaining fish. Break the cubes of cooked fish into smaller pieces and keep warm.

5. To assemble each taco, place 2 tablespoons of the lettuce in the center of a warm corn tortilla and top with about one-twelfth of the fish. Add 2 or 3 strips pickled jalapeño and 1 tablespoon pickled onions. Drizzle with 1 tablespoon of the crema. Serve with lime wedges.

MAKES 12 TACOS; SERVES 6

NUTRITIONAL ANALYSIS PER TACO
Calories 277 (Kilojoules 1,163); Protein 14 g; Carbohydrates 31 g; Total Fat 11 g; Saturated Fat 4 g; Cholesterol 36 mg; Sodium 200 mg; Dietary Fiber 2 g

Green Chile–Chicken Enchiladas

GREEN CHILE SAUCE

3 tablespoons olive oil or vegetable oil

1 white onion, finely chopped

2 cloves garlic, minced

1 teaspoon dried Mexican oregano

2 teaspoons coriander seed, toasted and ground *(page 141)*

1–2 tablespoons all-purpose (plain) flour (optional)

1½ cups (9 oz/280 g) roasted, peeled, seeded, and chopped New Mexico green chile *(page 138)*

2 cups (16 fl oz/500 ml) chicken stock

kosher salt to taste

3 cups (24 fl oz/750 ml) chicken stock

1 teaspoon dried Mexican oregano

1 bay leaf

1½ lb (750 g) skinless, boneless chicken breasts

kosher salt to taste

vegetable oil for frying

18 corn tortillas

3 cups (12 oz/375 g) shredded Monterey jack cheese

1 cup (2 oz/60 g) finely shredded romaine (cos) lettuce

1 cup (6 oz/185 g) diced ripe tomato

¾ cup (6 fl oz/180 ml) sour cream

This combination, topped with lots of melted cheese, is a favorite item on Southwestern menus.

1. To make the sauce, in a saucepan over medium heat, warm the oil. Add the onion and sauté until softened, about 5 minutes. Add the garlic, oregano, coriander, and the flour, if using, and stir to combine. Stir in the green chile and stock, season with salt, and cook uncovered, stirring frequently, until slightly thickened, 20–30 minutes. Set aside.

2. In a saucepan over medium-high heat, combine the stock, oregano, and bay leaf and bring to a boil. Add the chicken, reduce the heat to medium-low, and simmer for 10 minutes. Remove from the heat and let the chicken cool in the liquid. Remove the chicken and reserve the broth for another use. Shred the meat finely, sprinkle with salt, and set aside.

3. Preheat the oven to 350°F (180°C). Oil a 2½-qt (2.5-l) baking dish.

4. In a small frying pan over medium-high heat, pour in oil to a depth of ¾ inch (2 cm). When hot, using tongs, immerse a tortilla in the oil, turning once, for 3–4 seconds on each side. Drain on paper towels. Repeat with the remaining tortillas.

5. Lay 1 tortilla on a plate and place 2 tablespoons of the shredded chicken close to the edge. Roll up the tortilla and place, seam side down, in the prepared dish. Repeat until all the tortillas are filled. Ladle the chile sauce over the top. Bake until the sauce is bubbly and the enchiladas are heated through, 25–30 minutes. Remove from the oven and sprinkle with the cheese. Place an oven rack in the top position and return the enchiladas to the oven. Bake until the cheese melts, about 6 minutes.

6. Place 3 enchiladas on each warmed individual plate. Spoon the sauce from the dish over them, then sprinkle with the lettuce and tomato. Top with the sour cream and serve.

SERVES 6

NUTRITIONAL ANALYSIS PER SERVING
Calories 803 (Kilojoules 3,373); Protein 48 g; Carbohydrates 46 g; Total Fat 49 g; Saturated Fat 17 g; Cholesterol 138 mg; Sodium 940 mg; Dietary Fiber 6 g

Green Chile Stew

Commonly called simply *chile verde,* or "green chile," this easy-to-make, delicious dish is one of New Mexico's most popular traditional stews. Regional markets sell the state's green chiles both fresh and frozen. If you cannot find them, substitute Anaheim or poblano chiles, both close cousins.

1. In a large saucepan over high heat, warm the oil. In batches, add the pork and brown well on all sides, 6–8 minutes. Using a slotted spoon, transfer to a plate and set aside.

2. Add the onion to the oil remaining in the pan over medium-high heat and sauté until lightly golden, about 4 minutes. Add the garlic and sauté for 1 minute longer. Add the mushrooms and sauté until the edges are browned, 3–4 minutes. Add the potatoes, coriander, oregano, and bay leaves and return the meat to the pan. Stir well, pour in the stock, and add 1 teaspoon of the salt. Bring to a boil, reduce the heat to medium, and simmer, uncovered, until the meat is just tender, about 30 minutes.

3. Add the green chiles and continue to simmer, uncovered, for 20 minutes longer until the chiles are heated through and the meat is very tender. Stir in the remaining 1 teaspoon salt, then taste and adjust with more salt if necessary.

4. Ladle into warmed bowls and garnish with the crema or crème fraîche. Serve at once.

SERVES 6

NUTRITIONAL ANALYSIS PER SERVING
Calories 478 (Kilojoules 2,008); Protein 36 g; Carbohydrates 24 g; Total Fat 27 g; Saturated Fat 9 g; Cholesterol 114 mg; Sodium 1,631 mg; Dietary Fiber 3 g

3 tablespoons toasted peanut oil or vegetable oil

2 lb (1 kg) boneless pork shoulder or butt, trimmed of excess fat, cut into ¾-inch (2-cm) cubes

1 white onion, chopped

2 cloves garlic, minced

½ lb (250 g) white or brown fresh mushrooms, brushed clean and quartered through the stem end

¾ lb (375 g) small yellow-fleshed potatoes, quartered lengthwise

1½ teaspoons coriander seed, toasted and ground *(page 141)*

1 teaspoon dried Mexican oregano

2 bay leaves

6 cups (48 fl oz/1.5 l) chicken stock

2 teaspoons kosher salt, or to taste

12–16 New Mexico green chiles (about 2 lb/1 kg total), roasted, peeled, and seeded *(page 138),* then chopped (about 3 cups/18 oz/560 g)

6 tablespoons (3 fl oz/90 ml) crema or crème fraîche

Grilled Quail

MARINADE

1 large white onion, cut into large chunks

5 large cloves garlic

1 cup (8 fl oz/250 ml) cider vinegar

1 cup (8 fl oz/250 ml) water

3 tablespoons Worcestershire sauce

3 small *piloncillo* cones (1 oz/30 g each) or ¼ cup (2 oz/60 g) firmly packed dark brown sugar

2 tablespoons puréed chipotle chiles in adobo sauce

12 fresh tarragon sprigs

12 partially boned quail, wing bones snipped off

2–3 tablespoons olive oil

kosher salt and freshly ground pepper to taste

In the past, quail were among the most important game birds in the Southwest. Today, they are farm-raised and sold at specialty meat and poultry markets. You can purchase them partially boned (rib bones removed), which makes the birds easier to work with and to eat. *Piloncillo* is unrefined sugar from Mexico. It comes shaped in dark brown cones in sizes ranging from 1 to 12 ounces (30 to 375 g).

1. To make the marinade, in a food processor, combine the onion and garlic and pulse to form a coarse purée. Scrape the mixture into a non-aluminum saucepan and add the vinegar, water, Worcestershire sauce, *piloncillo* or brown sugar, chipotle purée, and tarragon. Bring to a boil over high heat, stirring to dissolve the sugar. Reduce the heat to medium and simmer for 5 minutes to blend the flavors. Let cool.

2. Pour the marinade into a nonaluminum bowl. Immerse the quail in the cool marinade, cover, and refrigerate for 4 hours.

3. Prepare a fire in a charcoal grill.

4. Remove the quail from the marinade and pat dry with paper towels. Strain the marinade through a medium-mesh sieve into a nonaluminum saucepan and place over medium heat. Bring to a simmer and cook until reduced and slightly thickened, 20–25 minutes. This will be the sauce for the quail. Rub the quail with the oil and season with salt and pepper.

5. Place the quail, breast side down, on the grill rack about 6 inches (15 cm) above the coals. Grill until the skin is browned and getting crisp, about 4 minutes. Turn and continue to grill until the breast is cooked but still pink when cut into with a knife, about 2 minutes longer.

6. Arrange 2 quail on each warmed individual plate and spoon 2–3 tablespoons of the sauce over each bird. Serve immediately.

SERVES 6

NUTRITIONAL ANALYSIS PER SERVING
Calories 536 (Kilojoules 2,251); Protein 44 g; Carbohydrates 17 g; Total Fat 32 g; Saturated Fat 8 g; Cholesterol 166 mg; Sodium 249 mg; Dietary Fiber 1 g

Chicken-Fried Steak with Chipotle Gravy

1½ lb (750 g) chuck steak, ½ inch (12 mm) thick, divided into 6 equal pieces

1½ cups (7½ oz/235 g) unbleached all-purpose (plain) flour

2 tablespoons ground ancho chile

1 tablespoon kosher salt

2 teaspoons freshly ground black pepper

2 teaspoons dried Mexican oregano

2 teaspoons cumin seed, toasted and ground *(page 141)*

peanut oil for frying

CHIPOTLE GRAVY

3 tablespoons unbleached all-purpose (plain) flour

1 cup (8 fl oz/250 ml) milk

1 cup (8 fl oz/250 ml) heavy (double) cream

2 teaspoons chopped fresh thyme

1 tablespoon sauce from chipotle chiles in adobo sauce, or to taste

½ teaspoon freshly ground white pepper

1 teaspoon coriander seed, toasted and ground *(page 141)*

kosher salt to taste

The Midwestern roots of Southwestern cuisine show up clearly in this home-style dish. Serve with warmed Flour Tortillas (page 86) or heaps of mashed potatoes.

1. One at a time, place the pieces of meat between sheets of plastic wrap and, using a meat pounder, pound the steaks to an even ¼-inch (6-mm) thickness. In a bowl, stir together the flour, ground chile, salt, black pepper, oregano, and cumin. Coat each steak with the seasoned flour, shaking off any excess.

2. Pour peanut oil to a depth of ¼ inch (6 mm) into a cast-iron frying pan and place over medium heat. Add the steaks to the hot oil and fry, turning once, until golden, 4–5 minutes on each side. Using tongs, transfer to paper towels to drain. Keep warm.

3. Discard all but 3 tablespoons of the oil from the pan. To make the gravy, return the pan to medium heat and stir in the flour. Cook, stirring, for 3 minutes without browning. Gradually whisk in the milk and cream and simmer until thickened, about 3 minutes. Stir in the thyme, adobo sauce, white pepper, and coriander and season with salt.

4. Place the steaks on warmed individual plates and ladle 4–6 tablespoons (2–3 fl oz/60–90 ml) gravy over each steak. Serve at once.

SERVES 6

NUTRITIONAL ANALYSIS PER SERVING
Calories 719 (Kilojoules 3,020); Protein 28 g; Carbohydrates 36 g; Total Fat 51 g; Saturated Fat 21 g; Cholesterol 144 mg; Sodium 847 mg; Dietary Fiber 2 g

Chile-Rubbed Cowboy Steak

RUB

2 large ancho chiles

¼ cup (¾ oz/20 g) ground ancho chile

3 tablespoons cumin seed, toasted and ground *(page 141)*

3 tablespoons coriander seed, toasted and ground *(page 141)*

¼ cup (2 fl oz/60 ml) puréed chipotle chiles in adobo sauce

6 cloves garlic, minced

1 bunch fresh cilantro (fresh coriander), coarsely chopped

2 tablespoons kosher salt

2 tablespoons freshly ground pepper

6 T-bone steaks, 1 lb (500 g) each

¼ cup (2 fl oz/60 ml) olive oil

kosher salt and freshly ground pepper to taste

The powerfully aromatic rub for these steaks is a variation of *adobada,* a spice mixture traditionally used to preserve meats. Tell your guests to bring along robust appetites for the big T-bones called for here, or substitute smaller steaks such as rib eyes or New York strips.

1. To make the rub, in a small dry frying pan over medium-high heat toast the ancho chiles, turning once, until fragrant, a few seconds on each side. Transfer them to a bowl, add hot water to cover, and let soak for 20 minutes. Lift out the chiles, reserving the soaking water, and remove the stems. In a food processor, combine the chiles and a little of the soaking water and purée until fairly smooth. The resulting sauce should be the consistency of thick heavy (double) cream. Press the purée through a medium-mesh sieve.

2. In the food processor, combine the puréed ancho chiles, the ground ancho, cumin, coriander, chipotle purée, garlic, cilantro, salt, and pepper. Process until a stiff paste forms. Add a little water, if needed, to facilitate processing.

3. Spread the rub evenly over both sides of the steaks, cover with plastic wrap, and refrigerate for 6 hours or up to overnight.

4. Remove the steaks from the refrigerator 30 minutes before grilling. Scrape most of the rub from the surface of the meat.

5. Prepare a fire in a charcoal grill, or preheat a stove-top grill pan over high heat. Brush the steaks with the olive oil and season with salt and pepper. Place the steaks on the grill rack or grill pan and grill, turning once, for 4–5 minutes on each side for medium-rare. Transfer to warmed individual plates and serve at once.

SERVES 6

NUTRITIONAL ANALYSIS PER SERVING
Calories 808 (Kilojoules 3,394); Protein 64 g; Carbohydrates 2 g; Total Fat 59 g; Saturated Fat 22 g; Cholesterol 210 mg; Sodium 546 mg; Dietary Fiber 1 g

Early in the sixteenth century, the Spanish brought to the New World two animals, the horse and the cow, that would radically change the lives of the people who lived there. Soon men on horseback were driving cattle north out of Mexico and into the American Southwest.

Along with the cattle, the *vaquero* (Mexican cowboy) brought his skills to the region, which the newly arrived Anglos adopted as their own, transforming themselves into the now-legendary Western cowboys. The first *ranchos,* homes of the original cattle barons, were quickly established near the Spanish missions.

In 1848, with the end of Spanish rule in the Southwest, the region attracted more Anglo settlers from the Midwest and East. The era of huge cattle drives to railheads, for delivery to slaughterhouses in the north, had begun. Slow travel and long distances between ranches and between towns made hospitality more of a necessity than a social grace. Tables were laid with hearty meals based on beef, beans, rice, corn, squash, tomatoes, chiles, and bread, and hospitality became yet another legend of the West.

Ranching Influence

Today, the Southwest remains an area where hearty ranch-style meals are still served to large gatherings. Barbecued meats, tasty stews, long-simmered beans, plump tamales, biscuits, sourdough breads and pancakes, fruit pies and crumbly cakes all speak of an earlier time, of the era of the rancho and the cowboy.

Beef Salpicón Tacos

3 tablespoons olive oil

1 beef brisket, 1½ lb (750 g)

1 small white onion, quartered
   through the stem end

1 small head garlic, halved horizontally

DRESSING

¼ cup (2 fl oz/60 ml) puréed chipotle
   chiles in adobo sauce

3–4 tablespoons (1½–2 fl oz/
   45–60 ml) cider vinegar

3 cloves garlic, minced

½ cup (4 fl oz/125 ml) olive oil

pinch of sugar, or to taste

kosher salt to taste

1 small red (Spanish) onion, cut into
   ¼-inch (6-mm) dice

4 ripe plum (Roma) tomatoes, cut
   into ½-inch (12-mm) cubes

2 ripe Haas avocados, pitted, peeled,
   and cut into ½-inch (12-mm) dice

⅓ cup (½ oz/15 g) coarsely chopped
   fresh cilantro (fresh coriander)

6 large radishes, thinly sliced

2 cups (4 oz/125 g) finely shredded
   romaine (cos) lettuce

24 corn tortillas, heated

In Mexico, *salpicón* is a salad or other well-seasoned mixture of shredded meat or seafood, made with beef in the north, pork in the south, and crabmeat along the coasts. Whatever the main ingredient, it makes a perfect casual filling for tacos, as this Southwestern version demonstrates. For a picnic, you could eliminate the tortillas, mix in all the garnishes, and serve the recipe as a salad.

1. In a large frying pan over medium-high heat, warm the olive oil. Add the brisket and brown well on all sides, 3–4 minutes on each side. Transfer the meat to a heavy pot and add the onion, garlic, and water to cover. Bring to a boil, cover, reduce the heat to low, and simmer until very tender, 1½–2 hours. Remove from the heat and let the meat cool in the stock. Remove the meat from the stock and reserve the stock for another use or discard it. Using 2 forks or your fingers, thinly shred the meat and set aside. (The recipe can be prepared up to this point 1 day in advance of serving.)

2. To make the dressing, in a small bowl, stir together the chipotle purée, vinegar, and garlic. Whisk the olive oil into the mixture and season with sugar and salt.

3. Place the onion, tomatoes, avocados, cilantro, radishes, and lettuce in small separate bowls and set out on the table. In a serving bowl, toss the shredded beef with the dressing and place on the table as well, along with the tortillas. Let your guests assemble their own tacos.

SERVES 6

NUTRITIONAL ANALYSIS PER SERVING
Calories 866 (Kilojoules 3,637); Protein 28 g; Carbohydrates 59 g; Total Fat 60 g;
Saturated Fat 15 g; Cholesterol 78 mg; Sodium 315 mg; Dietary Fiber 8 g

Marinated Rack of Lamb

Spaniards introduced the churro breed of sheep to the Southwest. Today, these prized free-range sheep thrive on the wild herbs and greens that flourish in the countryside, which makes their meat especially flavorful. The complex flavors of chile caribe accentuate the rich taste of lamb.

1. To make the marinade, in a food processor, combine the onions, garlic, oregano, cumin, coriander, and chile caribe or red pepper flakes. Pulse to form a coarse purée. With the motor running, pour in the olive oil. Season with salt and black pepper.

2. Coat the meaty parts of the racks with the marinade and place them in a baking dish. Cover and let stand at room temperature for 2 hours or for up to overnight in the refrigerator.

3. If you have refrigerated the meat, let it come to room temperature before continuing. Preheat the oven to 500°F (260°C). Line a baking sheet with aluminum foil.

4. Scrape the marinade from the lamb and discard. In a large, heavy frying pan over high heat, warm the olive oil. One at a time, brown the racks on both sides, about 5 minutes for each rack. As they are browned, transfer the racks to the prepared baking sheet.

5. Roast the lamb until done to your liking, 15–20 minutes for medium-rare. Remove from the oven and let rest for 10 minutes.

6. Cut the racks apart into double chops and place 2 double chops on each warmed individual plate. Serve immediately.

SERVES 6

NUTRITIONAL ANALYSIS PER SERVING
Calories 538 (Kilojoules 2,260); Protein 38 g; Carbohydrates 12 g; Total Fat 38 g; Saturated Fat 9 g; Cholesterol 122 mg; Sodium 124 mg; Dietary Fiber 2 g

MARINADE

2 large white onions, cut into chunks

1 large head garlic, cloves separated and peeled

1 tablespoon dried Mexican oregano

1 tablespoon cumin seed, toasted and ground (page 141)

1 tablespoon coriander seed, toasted and ground (page 141)

2 tablespoons chile caribe or 4 teaspoons red pepper flakes

½ cup (4 fl oz/125 ml) extra-virgin olive oil

kosher salt and freshly ground black pepper to taste

3 racks of lamb, 1½–2 lb (750 g–1 kg) each, trimmed of all fat and rib bones frenched

¼ cup (2 fl oz/60 ml) extra-virgin olive oil

Chiles Rellenos with Carne Adobada

CARNE ADOBADA

¼ cup (2 fl oz/60 ml) peanut oil

2 lb (1 kg) pork shoulder or butt, cut into ¾-inch (2-cm) cubes

1 large white onion, diced

2 large cloves garlic, minced

3 cups (24 fl oz/750 ml) chicken stock, or as needed

1 teaspoon each cumin and coriander seed, toasted and ground *(page 141)*

1 teaspoon dried Mexican oregano

½ cup (1½ oz/45 g) ground Chimayó chile

pinch of kosher salt, or to taste

CHILES RELLENOS

6 large New Mexico green chiles, roasted and peeled *(page 138)*

⅓ cup (3 fl oz/80 ml) gold tequila

6 tablespoons (2 oz/60 g) golden raisins (sultanas)

½ lb (250 g) fresh goat cheese

6 tablespoons (2 oz/60 g) piñon nuts or other pine nuts, toasted

kosher salt to taste

vegetable oil for deep-frying

½ cup (2½ oz/75 g) unbleached all-purpose (plain) flour

2 eggs, lightly beaten with 2 table-spoons water

cornmeal coating for Cornmeal-Crusted Trout *(page 76)*

steamed white rice, crema, and Fresh Tomato Salsa *(page 116)* (optional)

1. To make the *carne adobada,* in a large, heavy pot over medium-high heat, warm the oil. Working in batches, add the pork and brown well on all sides, 4–5 minutes. Transfer to a plate. Add the onion to the pot and sauté until golden, about 5 minutes. Add the garlic and cook for 1 minute until fragrant. Pour in 1 cup (8 fl oz/250 ml) of the stock and deglaze the pot, stirring to dislodge the browned bits.

2. Add the cumin, coriander, oregano, ground chile, and salt to the pot and mix well. Add the remaining 2 cups (16 fl oz/500 ml) stock, stirring until smooth. Return the pork cubes to the pot and bring to a boil. Reduce the heat to low, cover, and simmer until the pork is tender, about 1 hour. Add stock as needed to keep the meat covered at all times.

3. To make the chiles rellenos, make a slit lengthwise in each green chile and remove the ribs and seeds. Pour the tequila into a small frying pan, add the raisins, and bring to a boil. Reduce the heat and simmer briefly, then set aside for 10 minutes. In a small bowl, mix together the cheese, nuts, raisins and any unabsorbed tequila, and salt.

4. Line a baking sheet with paper towels. Fill each chile with 2–3 tablespoons of the cheese mixture and pinch closed. Place on the prepared baking sheet, cover, and refrigerate for at least 2 hours or up to overnight.

5. Pour vegetable oil to a depth of 3 inches (7.5 cm) into a deep, heavy saucepan and heat to 365°F (185°C). Meanwhile, coat each chile evenly with the flour, shaking off the excess, then dip in the egg mixture, and finally in the cornmeal coating, pressing lightly to adhere.

6. Slip 2 chiles into the hot oil and fry until golden, about 3 minutes. Drain on paper towels; keep warm. Repeat with the remaining chiles.

7. Place the chiles on warmed individual plates and top with a few pieces of the pork and some sauce. Serve with steamed white rice and pass crema and salsa at the table, if you like.

SERVES 6

NUTRITIONAL ANALYSIS PER SERVING
Calories 987 (Kilojoules 4,145); Protein 46 g; Carbohydrates 64 g; Total Fat 60 g; Saturated Fat 19 g; Cholesterol 196 mg; Sodium 1,522 mg; Dietary Fiber 8 g

Cornmeal-Crusted Trout with Corn Relish

CORN RELISH

4 ears of corn, husks and silk removed

1 small white onion, sliced ½ inch (12 mm) thick

1 small red bell pepper (capsicum), roasted, peeled, and seeded *(page 138),* then diced

1 large poblano chile, roasted, peeled, and seeded *(page 138),* then diced

¼ cup (⅓ oz/10 g) coarsely chopped fresh cilantro (fresh coriander)

1–2 tablespoons white wine vinegar

2–3 tablespoons toasted peanut oil

kosher salt to taste

CORNMEAL COATING

1½ cups (7½ oz/235 g) stone-ground yellow cornmeal

¼ cup (1½ oz/45 g) *masa harina*

6 tablespoons (1 oz/30 g) ground Chimayó chile

1½ teaspoons freshly ground coriander

1 teaspoon freshly ground cumin

1 tablespoon kosher salt

1 teaspoon freshly ground pepper

1 cup (5 oz/155 g) unbleached all-purpose (plain) flour

3 eggs

6 boneless whole trout

kosher salt and freshly ground pepper to taste

3 tablespoons olive oil

Mountain trout is one of the few fish varieties that exist in New Mexico's high desert. A town in the northeastern part of the state has even honored the much prized fish by taking its Spanish name, Truchas.

1. To make the relish, working with 1 ear of corn at a time and holding it with tongs, toast over a gas flame or under a broiler (griller) until evenly charred in spots. Let cool, then, steadying the stalk end on a cutting board, strip off the kernels with a sharp knife. There should be about 2 cups (12 oz/375 g). Char the onion slices in the same way, let cool, and chop finely. In a bowl, combine the corn, onion, bell pepper, chile, cilantro, and the vinegar, peanut oil, and salt to taste. Set aside.

2. Preheat the oven to 475°F (245°C). Line a baking sheet with aluminum foil.

3. To make the coating, in a bowl, combine the cornmeal, *masa harina*, ground chile, coriander, cumin, salt, and pepper. Whisk to combine. Transfer to a shallow dish large enough to accommodate 1 trout.

4. Spread the flour on a flat plate. Beat the eggs in a shallow dish large enough to accommodate 1 trout. Season each trout cavity with salt and pepper and dust the outside with the flour, shaking off the excess. Dip the trout into the beaten eggs, then coat it with the cornmeal, pressing lightly to adhere. Transfer to a rack and repeat with the remaining trout.

5. In a nonstick frying pan over medium-high heat, warm the oil. Add 2 trout and brown, turning once, for 1–2 minutes on each side. Transfer to the prepared baking sheet and repeat with the remaining trout.

6. Bake the trout until opaque throughout when pierced with a knife, about 5 minutes. Transfer to warmed individual plates, spoon some corn relish over each fish, and serve.

SERVES 6

NUTRITIONAL ANALYSIS PER SERVING
Calories 810 (Kilojoules 3,402); Protein 60 g; Carbohydrates 70 g; Total Fat 33 g;
Saturated Fat 6 g; Cholesterol 238 mg; Sodium 902 mg; Dietary Fiber 7 g

Texas Bowl o' Red

3 lb (1.5 kg) boneless beef chuck

2 tablespoons vegetable oil

1 large white onion, coarsely chopped

3 cloves garlic, minced

2–3 tablespoons ground New Mexico chile

2 bay leaves

1 tablespoon coriander seed, toasted and ground *(page 141)*

2 teaspoons cumin seed, toasted and ground *(page 141)*

2 teaspoons freshly ground canela or 1 teaspoon ground cinnamon

2 teaspoons dried Mexican oregano

1 can (28 oz/875 g) plum (Roma) tomatoes with juice, puréed

1 oz (30 g) bittersweet chocolate

pinch of sugar

1 tablespoon *masa harina* stirred into ¼ cup (2 fl oz/60 ml) water (optional)

kosher salt and freshly ground pepper to taste

sour cream

Taking its traditional cowboy name from the dried red chiles that give it color and fire, authentic Texas chili has as many variations as there are cooks who claim to make the best bowl in the state. Add more or less ground chile to make this classic beef-and-no-beans version as hot or as mild as you like. Serve with cooked pinto beans or black beans or Seasoned White Rice (page 94).

1. Trim any excess fat from the beef, then cut into ½-inch (12-mm) cubes. In a large saucepan over medium-high heat, warm the vegetable oil. Add the onion and sauté until softened, 3–4 minutes. Add the garlic and sauté for 1–2 minutes longer. Raise the heat to high and, in batches, add the beef and brown well on all sides, 8–10 minutes. Reduce the heat to medium and stir in the ground chile, bay leaves, coriander, cumin, canela or cinnamon, oregano, and the puréed tomatoes. Bring to a boil, reduce the heat to medium, and simmer uncovered, stirring frequently, until thickened, about 1 hour.

2. Add the chocolate, sugar, and the diluted *masa harina,* if you wish to thicken the stew slightly, and stir to combine. Cook for 15–20 minutes to blend the flavors. Taste and adjust the seasoning with salt and pepper.

3. Ladle into warmed bowls, garnish with a dollop of sour cream, and serve immediately.

SERVES 6

NUTRITIONAL ANALYSIS PER SERVING
Calories 707 (Kilojoules 2,969); Protein 42 g; Carbohydrates 15 g; Total Fat 54 g; Saturated Fat 21 g; Cholesterol 163 mg; Sodium 406 mg; Dietary Fiber 4 g

Most people consider politics and religion subjects too volatile to discuss in polite society. But when compared to a debate about "authentic" chili, both topics seem tame. Chili? Most Mexicans disdain it, every Texan claims it, and some folks are hard put even to agree that it contains meat and chiles.

Meat? The only choice is Texas beef, but then upstart chili cooks use pork, lamb, and even duck. Chiles? Everything is possible, whole and ground. Texans insist on red chiles, of course, thus the state nickname for the dish, bowl o' red. Beans? Not for any self-respecting Texan, but others add them without a second thought. Tomatoes? Maybe and maybe not.

Although most folks will never agree on what goes into an authentic chili, they have transferred some of the energy once devoted to those fierce exchanges to competing in chili cookoffs. The Chili Appreciation Society International remains the oldest group to sponsor these contests. It has sanctioned more than 450 cookoffs throughout North America, and winners go on to compete at the Terlingua International Chili Championship in Texas.

Texas **Chili**

Begun in 1967, the newer International Chili Society, whose members proudly sport the nickname chiliheads, holds more than 300 cookoffs worldwide, with more than one million people tasting, cooking, and judging. Each year a world championship is held, with such colorfully named winners as Nevada Annie and Tarantula Jack.

Pork with Red and Yellow Plum Tomato Salsa

MARINADE

3 tablespoons toasted peanut oil

2 white onions, diced

2 large cloves garlic, minced

2 tablespoons juniper berries, crushed and coarsely chopped

2 tablespoons chile caribe or 4 teaspoons red pepper flakes

2 teaspoons cumin seed, toasted and ground *(page 141)*

2 teaspoons dried Mexican oregano, crushed

1 teaspoon freshly ground canela or ½ teaspoon ground cinnamon

2–3 tablespoons honey

2 tablespoons sherry vinegar

2 tablespoons Worcestershire sauce

¾ cup (2¼ oz/67 g) ground Chimayó chile

½ cup (4 fl oz/125 ml) chicken stock or water

2 pork tenderloins, 12–14 oz (375–440 g) each, trimmed of excess fat

3 tablespoons toasted peanut oil

Fresh Tomato Salsa *(page 116),* using 1 cup (6 oz/185 g) each yellow and red baby plum (Roma) tomatoes in place of the cherry tomatoes

In small towns throughout the Southwest, pork is traditionally the centerpiece of major celebrations. This recipe highlights a choice cut, the tenderloin, with a sweet and spicy marinade and a zesty and colorful tomato salsa.

1. To make the marinade, in a large frying pan over medium-high heat, warm the oil. Add the onions and garlic and sauté until lightly golden, about 5 minutes. Add the juniper berries, chile caribe or red pepper flakes, cumin, oregano, canela or cinnamon, honey to taste, vinegar, and Worcestershire sauce. Stir well, then stir in the ground chile, mixing thoroughly. Add the chicken stock or water to thin slightly. The mixture should be thick enough to coat the pork. Let cool to room temperature.

2. Place the pork tenderloins in a baking dish or in a large lock-top plastic bag and add the marinade. Turn the tenderloins to coat well, seal the bag if using, and refrigerate for at least 3 hours or up to overnight.

3. Preheat the oven to 475°F (245°C). Line a baking sheet with aluminum foil.

4. In a large frying pan over medium-high heat, warm the peanut oil. Remove 1 tenderloin from the dish or bag and place in the frying pan. Sear the tenderloin on all sides until browned, about 2 minutes on each side. Place the pork on the prepared baking sheet. Repeat the procedure with the remaining tenderloin.

5. Roast the pork for about 10 minutes for medium but still slightly pink. The timing will depend on the thickness of the tenderloins. Remove from the oven and let rest for about 10 minutes.

6. Slice the tenderloins on the diagonal about ¼ inch (6 mm) thick. Arrange an equal number of slices on each warmed individual plate. Garnish with the salsa. Serve at once.

SERVES 6

NUTRITIONAL ANALYSIS PER SERVING
Calories 342 (Kilojoules 1,436); Protein 28 g; Carbohydrates 16 g; Total Fat 19 g; Saturated Fat 4 g; Cholesterol 71 mg; Sodium 133 mg; Dietary Fiber 3 g

3 Beans, Grains & Vegetables

From southern Colorado to western Texas, beans play an important role in the local diet. They are served refried alongside enchiladas, simmered with chiles to accompany a steak, or baked with ham hocks for a ranch supper. They join a legion of other side dishes built on grains and vegetables—sautéed squash and corn, potato salad, savory rice pudding—all standards of the Southwestern menu. No less indispensable to the regional meal are tortillas, flour and corn, eaten right off the griddle. And, of course, a table is never complete without the hot and cool, sweet and bold flavors of a fresh salsa.

Posole with Winter Vegetables

2 cups (1 lb/500 g) dried posole, soaked overnight in water and drained, or 1 lb (500 g) thawed frozen posole

2 white onions, coarsely chopped

2 large cloves garlic, chopped

1 tablespoon dried Mexican oregano

1 tablespoon chile caribe or 2 teaspoons red pepper flakes

½ cup (4 fl oz/125 ml) olive oil

2 small carrots, peeled and chopped

2 small parsnips, peeled and chopped

1 fennel bulb, stems and feathery tops trimmed and coarsely chopped

2 butternut squashes, about 1½ lb (750 g) each, halved, seeded, peeled, and cut into ½-inch (12-mm) cubes

1 can (28 oz/875 g) diced tomatoes with juice

8 cups (64 fl oz/2 l) chicken stock, plus more as needed

½ cup (4 fl oz/125 ml) dry white wine

2 teaspoons each cumin and coriander seed, toasted and ground (page 141)

large pinch of saffron threads

kosher salt to taste

¾–1 cup (6–8 fl oz/180–250 ml) crema or crème fraîche

¼ small head green cabbage, finely shredded

½ cup (¾ oz/20 g) coarsely chopped fresh cilantro (fresh coriander)

3 limes, cut into wedges

Throughout the Southwest, posole is served as a main-dish stew and as a side dish with burritos, enchiladas, and other tortilla-wrapped items. The same term refers to the main ingredient, kernels of field or dent corn that have been treated with slaked lime to soften their hulls. If you can't find dried or frozen posole, substitute similar canned white hominy.

1. In a large saucepan, combine the soaked posole, onions, garlic, oregano, and chile caribe or red pepper flakes with water to cover by 3 inches (7.5 cm). Bring to a boil over high heat, cover partially, reduce the heat to medium-low, and simmer until the posole has softened, about 1 hour.

2. In a large saucepan over medium heat, warm the olive oil. Add the carrots, parsnips, and fennel and sauté until slightly softened, about 5 minutes. Add the squashes and continue to cook, stirring, for 2 minutes. Add the tomatoes, 8 cups (64 fl oz/2 l) stock, wine, cumin, coriander, saffron, and salt, raise the heat to high, and bring to a boil. Add the posole and its cooking liquid, reduce the heat to medium-low, and simmer uncovered, stirring frequently, until the vegetables are tender, about 1 hour. If the stew seems too thick, add more stock to thin to desired consistency. Taste and adjust the seasoning.

3. Ladle into warmed bowls and garnish each serving with the crema or crème fraîche, cabbage, and cilantro. Serve the posole immediately. Pass the lime wedges at the table.

SERVES 10–12

NUTRITIONAL ANALYSIS PER SERVING
Calories 437 (Kilojoules 1,835); Protein 9 g; Carbohydrates 58 g; Total Fat 21 g; Saturated Fat 6 g; Cholesterol 16 mg; Sodium 905 mg; Dietary Fiber 7 g

Flour Tortillas

2 cups (10 oz/315 g) unbleached all-purpose (plain) flour, plus extra if necessary for kneading

½ cup (2½ oz/75 g) *panocha* flour or whole-wheat (wholemeal) flour

1 teaspoon baking powder

1 teaspoon kosher salt

5 tablespoons (2½ oz/75 g) chilled lard or vegetable shortening

¾–1 cup (6–8 fl oz/180–250 ml) warm water, or as needed

Not so long ago, no store-bought tortilla could compare with homemade, but the quality of some commercial products continues to improve. The nice thing about making tortillas yourself, however, is the wonderful aroma that fills the kitchen as you cook them.

1. In a food processor, combine the flours, baking powder, and salt. Pulse a few times to mix. Add the lard or shortening and pulse to incorporate well. With the motor running, slowly add the warm water through the feed tube, adding only enough water and processing only long enough for the dough to come together into a ball.

2. Transfer the dough to a lightly floured surface and knead for 20 seconds. It should be a cohesive mass. If it feels too sticky, add a tablespoon or so more flour. Shape into a ball, cover with plastic wrap, and let rest for 20 minutes.

3. Divide the dough in half, then divide each half into 6 equal portions. Form each portion into a ball. Cover the balls with plastic wrap to keep them from drying out. On the lightly floured work surface, roll out a ball of dough into a round about 5 inches (13 cm) in diameter and ⅛ inch (3 mm) thick. Cover with plastic wrap. Repeat with the remaining balls.

4. Place a large cast-iron pan over medium-high heat. When it is hot, add 2 or 3 dough rounds and cook until bubbles appear on the surface and the underside looks dry and is speckled with brown, about 3 minutes. Turn the tortillas and cook on the second side for about 2 minutes. The tortillas will be slightly puffed and pliable. As they are done, wrap them in a kitchen towel to keep them warm. (If not serving right away, let cool, place in a plastic bag, and refrigerate overnight. Just before serving, wrap the tortillas in aluminum foil and reheat in a 350°F/180°C oven for 15 minutes.)

MAKES 12 TORTILLAS

NUTRITIONAL ANALYSIS PER TORTILLA
Calories 164 (Kilojoules 689); Protein 3 g; Carbohydrates 23 g; Total Fat 6 g; Saturated Fat 2 g; Cholesterol 6 mg; Sodium 236 mg; Dietary Fiber 1 g

Corn and flour tortillas serve as the main bread for Southwestern meals, but their use doesn't stop there. A tortilla can turn up as a base, a wrap, an ingredient, or a garnish. Cooks use them to make burritos, tacos, enchiladas, tostadas, soups, casseroles, egg dishes, and even desserts, and they range in size from no broader than a teacup to the large, nearly translucent Sonoran-style flour tortillas that can reach up to 18 inches (45 cm) in diameter.

Early cooks in the region prepared tortillas from the locally cultivated corn. The tortillas were made then, as they are today, from freshly prepared *masa* (dough) or from *masa harina* (flour made from processed dried corn) mixed with water. At a young age, cooks learned the traditional art of patting balls of dough into thin disks by hand or with the help of a tortilla press and then cooking them on a dry cast-iron griddle or frying pan.

The Spanish brought wheat to the Southwest and with it the flour tortilla, which remains popular in northern Mexico, where wheat fields sometimes stretch as far as the eye can see. The dough contains only

Tortillas

flour, a little lard, salt, and water. It is shaped into small balls, which are then transformed into rounds of varying size with the aid of a rolling pin or by stretching with lightly greased hands. Some are as thin as a sheet of tissue, others are thicker and puffy, and like corn tortillas, they are cooked on a dry griddle or in a frying pan.

Fresh Corn Pudding

8 ears of corn, husks and silk removed

1 can (15 fl oz/470 ml) evaporated milk

4 eggs, lightly beaten

¼ cup (2 oz/60 g) unsalted butter

1 white onion, chopped

2 cloves garlic, minced

1½ cups (5 oz/150 g) crushed rich cracker crumbs

1 cup (4 oz/120 g) shredded sharp cheddar cheese

sugar to taste, if needed

kosher salt and freshly ground pepper to taste

From July through September, bins at the Santa Fe farmers' market are piled high with fresh sweet corn, and I can't seem to get enough of it. I usually simply boil the just-picked ears and slather them with butter. For a change of pace, however, I sometimes turn the cut kernels into a simple pudding that I serve alongside Chile-Rubbed Cowboy Steak (page 70) or Marinated Rack of Lamb (page 73).

1. Preheat the oven to 350°F (180°C). Butter a 2-qt (2-l) baking dish.

2. Working with 1 ear of corn at a time, steady the stalk end on a cutting board and strip off the kernels with a knife. You should have about 4 cups (1½ lb/750 g).

3. In a blender, combine 3 cups (18 oz/560 g) of the corn kernels and the evaporated milk and purée until smooth. Pass the purée through a medium-mesh sieve placed over a bowl. Stir the eggs into the purée.

4. In a frying pan over medium-high, melt the butter. Add the onion and garlic and sauté until softened, about 3 minutes. Add the sautéed mixture to the puréed corn and stir to combine. Stir in the reserved 1 cup (6 oz/190 g) corn kernels, 1 cup (3 oz/90 g) of the cracker crumbs, and ½ cup (2 oz/60 g) of the cheese. Season with the sugar, if needed, salt, and pepper. Pour the mixture into the prepared baking dish and sprinkle with the remaining ½ cup (2 oz/60 g) cheese and ½ cup (2 oz/60 g) cracker crumbs.

5. Bake the corn pudding until set and golden, 45–50 minutes. Remove from the oven and let stand for 5 minutes. Spoon onto warmed individual plates to serve.

SERVES 6

NUTRITIONAL ANALYSIS PER SERVING
Calories 510 (Kilojoules 2,146); Protein 20 g; Carbohydrates 45 g; Total Fat 30 g; Saturated Fat 15 g; Cholesterol 207 mg; Sodium 432 mg; Dietary Fiber 5 g

Southwest
Trinity

The Southwest's early Pueblo Indians relied on a trinity of cultivated foods—corn, beans, and squash—for their daily sustenance. They supplemented this diet with small game and plants and later with new ingredients brought by Hispanic and Anglo explorers and settlers. But the trinity never lost its prominence, and corn, beans, and squash remain at the center of the Southwestern table.

In the past, corn was arguably the most important member of the trinity, and the earliest cultivated varieties came in a full spectrum of colors: creamy white, bright yellow, deep blue, and crimson red. Even today, a Southwestern meal without corn is almost unimaginable, and many contemporary cooks use tried-and-true family recipes—corn and tomato salsa, cornmeal-crusted trout, corn cakes, corn bread stuffing—that showcase this versatile staple.

Dried corn, treated with a modern version of the ash solution that the ancients used to remove the transparent skin covering each kernel, continues to play a central role. When boiled, the kernels, known as hominy outside the Southwest, become posole, a specialty of New Mexico and also the name for a hearty stew made from the treated corn. When soaked and ground, the kernels are transformed into *masa harina,* the flour for tortillas and tamales.

Like corn, beans have been cultivated in the Southwest for centuries. Today, such common beans as pinto, black, pink, and red flow into the Southwest from other states, ending up in stew pots and wrapped in tortillas. They join the local bolita, an heirloom variety well adapted to the high altitudes of New Mexico and Colorado; the various varieties of tepary bean—Jacob's cattle, painted pony, Raquel—that, because of long taproots, grow well in the desert; and the Anasazi, a slender, curved purple-white bean named for the ancient civilization of cliff dwellers that once flourished in the region.

This diversity is also found in the world of squashes. Thin-skinned yellow and green summer varieties called *calabacitas,* "little squashes," lend their name to a traditional New Mexican dish with corn and chiles. These same squashes supply blossoms, too, which Southwesterners were slipping into quesadillas and other dishes long before the flowers became fashionable ingredients.

With the arrival of late fall and winter, thick-skinned winter squashes and pumpkins are cooked up into a tableful of heartier dishes, their rich-colored flesh brightening the seasons' shorter days and colder nights.

Southwest cooking continues to evolve with a ready embrace of new ideas. At the same time, tradition is a mighty force, and the true regional cook would never be without a supply of corn, beans, and squashes, the Southwestern culinary trinity.

Brightly colored heirloom beans, including Anasazi, Appaloosa, and Black Runner, are enjoying a resurgence in popularity, as are squash blossoms, which add color and subtle flavor to dishes (opposite). A testimony to the versatility of corn (below): blue, white, and yellow corn flour; dried yellow corn kernels; and blue and white posole.

Golden Squash Purée with Garlic and Onions

ROASTED GARLIC

3 heads garlic

3 tablespoons olive oil

kosher salt and freshly ground pepper to taste

2 tablespoons water

SQUASH PURÉE

3 lb (1.5 kg) winter squashes such as butternut or small Hubbard, halved lengthwise and seeded

3 tablespoons extra-virgin olive oil

kosher salt and freshly ground pepper to taste

CARAMELIZED ONIONS

3 small red (Spanish) onions, cut through the root end into 6 wedges

3 tablespoons balsamic vinegar

3 tablespoons extra-virgin olive oil

kosher salt and freshly ground pepper to taste

¼ cup (2 oz/60 g) unsalted butter

1. Preheat the oven to 400°F (200°C). To prepare the roasted garlic, cut off the top third of each garlic head and discard. Stand the garlic heads upright in the center of an 8-inch (20-cm) square of aluminum foil. Drizzle with the olive oil, season with salt and pepper, and sprinkle with the water. Loosely seal the foil closed. Place on the oven rack and roast until soft and slightly caramelized, about 1½ hours. Set aside. (This will make about 6 tablespoons/2 oz/60 g roasted garlic.)

2. Reduce the oven temperature to 375°F (190°C). Line a baking sheet with aluminum foil. Place the squash halves, cut side up, on the prepared baking sheet. Drizzle with the olive oil and season with salt and pepper. Place in the oven and bake until the squashes are soft when pierced, about 1½ hours. Set aside to cool.

3. Raise the oven temperature to 400°F (200°C). Line another baking sheet with aluminum foil. To prepare the onions, in a bowl, toss the onion wedges with the vinegar, oil, salt, and pepper. Pour the onions and the liquid onto the prepared baking sheet. Roast until caramelized and the edges are crisp, 12–15 minutes. Remove from the oven and let cool. With small scissors, snip off the root end holding the layers of onion together on each wedge. Set the onion pieces aside.

4. Using a large spoon, scoop the flesh from the squash halves. Put half of the flesh in a food processor and purée until very smooth. Transfer to a bowl. Repeat with the remaining squash.

5. In a saucepan over medium heat, melt the butter. Add the squash purée and then squeeze the roasted garlic from its papery sheaths into the purée. Add the caramelized onion pieces and stir gently to incorporate all of the ingredients and heat through.

6. Transfer to a warmed bowl and serve at once.

SERVES 6

NUTRITIONAL ANALYSIS PER SERVING
Calories 375 (Kilojoules 1,575); Protein 5 g; Carbohydrates 30 g; Total Fat 29 g; Saturated Fat 8 g; Cholesterol 21 mg; Sodium 21 mg; Dietary Fiber 5 g

Seasoned White Rice

2 tablespoons olive oil or vegetable oil

1 cup (7 oz/220 g) long-grain white or basmati rice

1 small yellow onion, chopped

2 bay leaves

1 teaspoon salt

1½ cups (12 fl oz/375 ml) water

This bay-scented rice makes an aromatic accompaniment to nearly any main dish. Southwestern cooks borrowed the Mexican technique of sautéing rice before steaming it, a method that almost guarantees perfect and flavorful results every time. To make yellow rice, add 1 teaspoon dried safflower (the petals of the safflower thistle, available where Mexican ingredients are sold) with the onion and proceed as directed. To make red rice, add 1–2 teaspoons ground New Mexico chile with the onion.

1. In a 2-qt (2-l) saucepan over medium heat, warm the oil. Add the rice and stir until the grains turn opaque, 3–4 minutes. Add the onion, bay leaves, and salt and continue to stir until the rice is light tan, 2–3 minutes longer.

2. Add the water, stir well, and bring to a boil. Cover the pot, reduce the heat to low, and cook until all the liquid has been absorbed and the rice is tender, 25–30 minutes. Uncover, stir the rice, re-cover, remove from the heat, and let "steam" for 5 minutes longer.

3. Fluff the rice with a fork, discard the bay leaves, and transfer to a serving dish. Serve immediately.

MAKES ABOUT 3 CUPS (15 OZ/470 G); SERVES 6

NUTRITIONAL ANALYSIS PER SERVING
Calories 168 (Kilojoules 706); Protein 3 g; Carbohydrates 28 g; Total Fat 5 g; Saturated Fat 1 g; Cholesterol 0 mg; Sodium 391 mg; Dietary Fiber 1 g

Before the arrival of the Spaniards and the Mexicans, the Southwest's Native Americans flavored their daily fare with the wild herbs, roots, and grasses that grew around them. The outsiders introduced a trove of spices, however, and the locals soon adopted the exotic seasonings. Today, these "imports" continue to play a significant role in Southwestern cooking.

Among the new seasonings were cumin, coriander, and clove, as well as the following trio of more unusual ones.

Achiote **paste** is made from the pulp that surrounds the brick red seeds found in the fruits of the annatto tree, which is native to tropical America and the West Indies. The mildly peppery pulp colors whatever dish it flavors, usually meats, poultry, or seafood, a brilliant golden orange. It is sold as a dark red paste in small, solid blocks.

Canela refers to a specific variety of cinnamon from Sri Lanka. Also known as Mexican or Ceylon cinnamon, it tastes sweeter and more delicate and is softer and less costly than the more common Indian cinnamon. For the best flavor, buy the bark and freshly grind it in a spice grinder.

A Trio of **Spices**

Saffron is stigmas harvested from a type of crocus native to Asia Minor. It is sold as threads and powder, although the latter should be avoided as it can be easily adulterated. The pricey spice, called *azafrán* in Spanish, has a pleasantly bitter flavor and imparts a yellow-orange hue to foods. Dried safflower, an affordable alternative, will provide similar color.

Hearty Greens with Garlic and Chile Caribe

1 lb (500 g) collard greens, tough
    stems removed

1 lb (500 g) kale, tough stems
    removed

1 lb (500 g) mustard greens, tough
    stems removed

3 tablespoons plus 1 teaspoon toasted
    peanut oil or olive oil

¼ cup (2 fl oz/60 ml) water, or as
    needed

3 large cloves garlic, thinly sliced

2 teaspoons chile caribe or
    1½ teaspoons red pepper flakes,
    or to taste

kosher salt to taste

splash of red wine vinegar or balsamic
    vinegar

The renewed appreciation for robust and nutritious leafy vegetables such as kale, mustard greens, and collard greens gets a Southwestern twist here through the addition of a touch of chile caribe.

1. Cut all the greens crosswise into strips ½ inch (12 mm) wide. In a large frying pan over medium heat, warm the 3 tablespoons oil. Add the collard greens and ¼ cup (2 fl oz/60 ml) water, cover, and cook until the greens have softened, about 5 minutes. Add the kale, re-cover, and cook until the kale is wilted, about 5 minutes, adding a little more water if needed. Finally, add the mustard greens and cook, uncovered, until the greens are tender and the water has evaporated, 8–10 minutes longer.

2. Just before the greens are ready, in a small frying pan over medium-high heat, warm the 1 teaspoon oil. Add the garlic and sauté until just golden, about 1 minute. Remove from the heat and add the chile caribe or red pepper flakes.

3. Pour the garlic mixture over the cooked greens and toss to combine well. Transfer to a platter, season with salt, and add a splash of vinegar. Serve at once.

SERVES 6–8

NUTRITIONAL ANALYSIS PER SERVING
Calories 108 (Kilojoules 454); Protein 4 g; Carbohydrates 10 g; Total Fat 7 g;
Saturated Fat 1 g; Cholesterol 0 mg; Sodium 47 mg; Dietary Fiber 3 g

Native American Fry Bread

3 cups (15 oz/470 g) unbleached all-purpose (plain) flour

1 tablespoon baking powder

1 teaspoon kosher salt

3 tablespoons lard or vegetable shortening, at room temperature

1 cup (8 fl oz/250 ml) plus 1–2 tablespoons warm water or milk

vegetable oil for frying

Reminiscent of sopaipillas (page 134), this deep-fried bread is a staple among the Navajos and other Native Americans of the Southwest. The simple recipe goes nicely with stews, torn into pieces to sop up the juices. Eat the fry bread within 1 hour of making it for the best flavor and texture.

1. In a food processor, combine the flour, baking powder, and salt. Pulse a few times to mix. Add the lard or shortening and pulse to incorporate well. With the motor running, slowly pour in the warm water or milk through the feed tube, adding only enough liquid and processing only long enough for the dough to come together into a ball.

2. Transfer the dough to a lightly floured work surface and knead until smooth and elastic, about 10 minutes. Shape into a ball, cover with plastic wrap, and let rest for 20 minutes.

3. Divide the dough into 6 equal portions. On the lightly floured surface, roll out each portion into a round about ¼ inch (6 mm) thick. In a heavy saucepan or a deep, heavy frying pan, pour in vegetable oil to a depth of 3–4 inches (7.5–10 cm) and heat to 365°F (185°C) on a deep-frying thermometer. Add a dough round and fry, turning once, until puffed and golden, about 1 minute on each side. Using tongs, transfer to paper towels to drain; keep warm. Repeat with the remaining rounds, frying them one at a time. Serve warm.

SERVES 6

NUTRITIONAL ANALYSIS PER SERVING
Calories 407 (Kilojoules 1,709); Protein 8 g; Carbohydrates 57 g; Total Fat 16 g; Saturated Fat 4 g; Cholesterol 6 mg; Sodium 491 mg; Dietary Fiber 2 g

Calabacitas

3 tablespoons olive oil or unsalted butter, plus more oil or butter as needed

1 white onion, finely chopped

1 clove garlic, minced

2 small yellow summer squashes, trimmed and cut into ½-inch (12-mm) cubes

2 small green zucchini (courgettes), trimmed and cut into ½-inch (12-mm) cubes

1 small chayote, cut into ½-inch (12-mm) cubes

1 cup (6 oz/185 g) fresh or thawed frozen corn kernels

2 or 3 New Mexico green chiles, roasted, peeled, and seeded *(page 138),* then chopped (about ½ cup/3 oz/90 g)

¼ cup (⅓ oz/10 g) coarsely chopped fresh cilantro (fresh coriander) (optional)

kosher salt and freshly ground pepper to taste

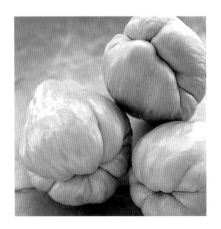

Although the name is Spanish, meaning "little squashes," this traditional New Mexican vegetable dish can be traced back to the tables of the early Native Americans, for whom its blend of summer squash, corn, and chiles was a staple. If you can't find the chayote, a native Mexican squash also known as vegetable pear and mirliton, substitute another yellow squash or zucchini. Serve with Pork with Red and Yellow Plum Tomato Salsa (page 80) or Skirt Steak Fajitas with Avocado Salsa (page 52).

1. In a frying pan over medium-high heat, warm 3 tablespoons of the oil or butter. Add the onion and sauté until softened, about 3 minutes. Add the garlic and sauté for 1 minute longer. Transfer the onion and garlic to a bowl. In batches, add the yellow squashes, zucchini, and chayote and sauté until softened and lightly golden, 5–6 minutes for the yellow squashes and zucchini and about 8 minutes for the chayote. Add more oil or butter as needed to prevent scorching. As the vegetables are ready, transfer them to the bowl holding the onion and garlic. Keep warm.

2. Add another tablespoon oil or butter to the frying pan over medium-high heat. Add the corn and sauté until it turns a deeper yellow, 3–4 minutes. Add the green chiles and continue to cook, stirring, for 3 minutes. Transfer the corn and chiles to the bowl holding the squashes.

3. Stir the vegetables to combine well, then mix in the cilantro, if using. Season with salt and pepper and serve immediately.

SERVES 6

NUTRITIONAL ANALYSIS PER SERVING
Calories 159 (Kilojoules 668); Protein 3 g; Carbohydrates 13 g; Total Fat 12 g;
Saturated Fat 2 g; Cholesterol 0 mg; Sodium 11 mg; Dietary Fiber 2 g

The Southwest's earliest inhabitants were faced with a hostile environment, a world of sandstorms and flash floods, heat waves and blizzards, little rain and scarce vegetation. Yet long before the first outsiders arrived, these Native Americans had carved out lives as desert farmers, hunters, and gatherers.

Contemporary Southwestern cooking owes much to these culinary forerunners. The most important crops of the past, corn, beans, and squash, continue to appear in every true Southwestern meal, turning up in such dishes as corn pudding, squash blossom quesadillas, and ranch-style beans.

The plants, game, and nuts once gathered in the wild only by Native Americans are now used by everyone. Purslane, a fleshy-leaved plant hardy enough to flourish in the most severe weather, goes into salads or vegetable dishes. Cactus paddles are added to side dishes, salads, and main courses, and cactus fruits are made into desserts. Spicy marinades coat grilled quail, birds hunted in the past and now farmed. Still-wild piñon nuts are used in chiles rellenos and punctuate everyday desserts.

Native Traditions

As new ingredients and ideas arrived, Native Americans incorporated them into their repertoire, using wheat for Indian fry bread or mastering smoking techniques for preserving the local trout. Today, Native Americans are still preparing their traditional dishes and creating new ones, and other Southwest cooks are continuing to learn from them.

Texas Potato Salad

DRESSING

⅓ cup (3 fl oz/80 ml) cider vinegar

⅓ cup (3 fl oz/80 ml) safflower oil
or vegetable oil

¼ cup (2 fl oz/60 ml) mayonnaise

1 small white onion, diced

2 small cloves garlic, minced

1 tablespoon juice from sweet gherkins

1 tablespoon yellow mustard

1 tablespoon sugar

1 teaspoon kosher salt

2 lb (1 kg) new potatoes, unpeeled

kosher salt and freshly ground pepper
to taste

3 hard-boiled eggs, peeled and coarsely
chopped

4 small sweet gherkins, finely diced

⅓ cup (2 oz/60 g) diced roasted red
bell pepper (capsicum) *(page 138)*

1 celery stalk, finely diced (optional)

5 green (spring) onions, including
tender green tops, thinly sliced
on the diagonal

3 tablespoons chopped fresh flat-leaf
(Italian) parsley

It comes as no surprise to even the most casual observer that Texans like their potatoes. A classic salad such as this one, with its mixture of mild and tangy, soft and crunchy ingredients, makes a perfect foil for more assertively seasoned main courses cooked on the backyard grill.

1. To make the dressing, in a blender, combine the vinegar, oil, mayonnaise, onion, garlic, gherkin juice, mustard, sugar, and salt. Blend until thoroughly emulsified. Taste and adjust the seasoning. Set aside.

2. In a saucepan, combine the potatoes with water to cover by 2–3 inches (5–7.5 cm). Bring to a boil and boil until tender, 25–35 minutes. Drain well and when just cool enough to handle, cut into slices ¼ inch (6 mm) thick or into 1-inch (2.5-cm) chunks. Place in a bowl and, while the potatoes are still warm, pour about one-third of the dressing over them. Season with salt and pepper and toss gently.

3. Add the hard-boiled eggs, gherkins, roasted bell pepper, celery (if using), green onions, and parsley to the potatoes. Add the remaining dressing and toss to coat evenly. Serve at room temperature, or cover and refrigerate to chill slightly before serving.

SERVES 6

NUTRITIONAL ANALYSIS PER SERVING
Calories 373 (Kilojoules 1,566); Protein 7 g; Carbohydrates 38 g; Total Fat 22 g; Saturated Fat 3 g; Cholesterol 112 mg; Sodium 505 mg; Dietary Fiber 3 g

Tart and Tangy Coleslaw

DRESSING

¼ cup (2 fl oz/60 ml) cider vinegar

2 tablespoons sugar

½–¾ teaspoon kosher salt

2 teaspoons hot-pepper sauce,
   or to taste

¾ lb (375 g) green cabbage, finely
   shredded

2 carrots, peeled and cut into thin
   julienne 1 inch (2.5 cm) long

½ red bell pepper (capsicum),
   seeded and cut lengthwise into
   narrow strips

½ yellow bell pepper (capsicum),
   seeded and cut lengthwise into
   narrow strips

6 large red radishes, trimmed and
   cut into thin julienne 1 inch
   (2.5 cm) long

2 tablespoons chopped fresh herbs
   such as cilantro (fresh coriander),
   mint, tarragon, and basil

European settlers carried coleslaw into the Southwest along the Santa Fe Trail. The region has made the dish its own by adding such ingredients as bell peppers, spicy radishes (a Mexican favorite), mint, and cilantro. Offer it as a cooling companion to spicy grilled meat or poultry.

1. To make the dressing, in a small bowl, whisk together the vinegar, sugar, salt to taste, and hot-pepper sauce. Let stand for several minutes to dissolve the sugar fully.

2. In a bowl, toss together the cabbage, carrots, bell peppers, and radishes. Pour the dressing over the vegetables, add the herbs, and toss well. Serve immediately.

SERVES 6

NUTRITIONAL ANALYSIS PER SERVING
Calories 47 (Kilojoules 197); Protein 1 g; Carbohydrates 11 g; Total Fat 0 g;
Saturated Fat 0 g; Cholesterol 0 mg; Sodium 219 mg; Dietary Fiber 3 g

Deserts, with their limited rainfall, temperature extremes, strong winds, and sparse vegetation and animal life, define great swaths of the Southwest. From the beginning, this harsh terrain dared the people who lived here to survive, to fashion shelter, to grow and gather food in an unforgiving environment.

All four of North America's deserts reach into the Southwest. The Sonoran travels north over the Mexican border into southwestern Arizona, and on the west, the Mojave extends a pair of narrow fingers into northwestern and west-central Arizona. The huge Chihuahuan, most of which lies in Mexico, edges into western Texas and southern New Mexico, and the even larger Great Basin, the most northern of the continent's deserts, spills into southwestern Colorado and northeastern Arizona.

Plant life varies in these dry lands, and each desert has its symbol: the saguaro in the Sonoran, the Joshua tree in the Mojave, the agave in the Chihuahuan, and the sagebrush in the Great Basin. But there are also creosote bushes and piñon trees, nopals and chollas, bursage and yucca.

Southwest Deserts

As water delivery methods improved, Southwest farmers successfully began claiming part of the desert for cropland. But today, both farmland and desert are losing ground to real estate developers. Now, the battle is no longer waged against the harshness of the desert but rather against the "progress" that many believe will destroy it.

"Refried" Black Beans

2⅛ cups (1 lb/500 g) dried black beans

1 tablespoon dried epazote

1 teaspoon dried thyme

1 teaspoon dried rosemary

¼ cup (2 fl oz/60 ml) olive oil

3 or 4 morita chiles

2 small white onions, chopped

2 cloves garlic, minced

½ lb (250 g) piece smoked pork
shank (optional)

1 teaspoon cumin seed, toasted and
ground (page 141)

1½ teaspoons coriander seed, toasted
and ground (page 141)

1 teaspoon freshly ground canela or
½ teaspoon ground cinnamon

pinch of ground allspice or ground
cloves

4 cups (32 fl oz/1 l) water, or more
if needed

6 cups (48 fl oz/1.5 l) chicken stock,
or more if needed

2–3 teaspoons cider vinegar or sherry
vinegar

1–2 teaspoons kosher salt

2–3 tablespoons toasted peanut oil
or olive oil

Black beans are not native to the Southwest, but they are
a pantry staple, ready for transforming into this creamy side
dish popular from Colorado to Texas.

1. Pick over the beans, discarding any stones, and rinse well. Place in a
bowl with water to cover by 2 inches (5 cm) and let stand overnight.

2. The next day, drain the beans and set aside. Crush the epazote, thyme,
and rosemary and set aside. In a heavy, 6-qt (6-l) pot over medium-high
heat, warm the ¼ cup (2 fl oz/60 ml) olive oil. Add the chiles and toast
until puffed and fragrant, about 30 seconds. Flip the chiles and toast on the
second side in the same way. Add the onions and garlic and cook, stirring,
until softened, 3–4 minutes. Add the pork shank (if using), the crushed
dried herbs, cumin, coriander, canela or cinnamon, allspice or cloves, beans,
and the 4 cups (32 fl oz/1 l) water. Stir well and bring to a boil over high
heat. Reduce the heat to medium-low and simmer uncovered, stirring
occasionally, until the beans are tender, 1–2 hours. The timing will depend
on the age of the beans. As the beans cook, gradually add the 6 cups
(48 fl oz/ 1.5 l) stock as needed to keep them always covered with liquid.

3. Add the vinegar and salt to taste and simmer for a few minutes
longer. Remove the pork shank, if used, and reserve for another use.
Discard the chiles, if desired.

4. In a large frying pan over medium heat, warm the peanut or olive
oil. Add half of the beans with their cooking liquid and mash with the
back of a wooden spoon, adding more water or stock if necessary to
keep them moist. They do not need to be smooth. Stir over medium heat
until nicely thickened, about 5 minutes, adding more liquid as needed to
achieve a mashed potato consistency.

5. Transfer to a serving bowl and serve at once.

SERVES 8–10

NUTRITIONAL ANALYSIS PER SERVING
Calories 297 (Kilojoules 1,247); Protein 13 g; Carbohydrates 36 g; Total Fat 12 g;
Saturated Fat 2 g; Cholesterol 0 mg; Sodium 918 mg; Dietary Fiber 8 g

Savory Rice Pudding

You'd be likely to find this hearty dish on the table at a Southwestern church supper. Full of satisfying flavors, it makes a great dish for entertaining, as it can be prepared ahead of time, refrigerated, and then baked the next day.

1. To make the tomato sauce, in a saucepan over medium-high heat, warm the oil. Add the onion and sauté until softened, about 3 minutes. Add the garlic and continue to sauté until lightly golden, 3–4 minutes. Add the chile strips, the puréed and diced tomatoes and their juice, oregano, and bay leaf and stir to combine thoroughly. Taste and season with sugar, salt, and pepper. Simmer uncovered, stirring occasionally, until slightly thickened, about 20 minutes. Set aside.

2. Meanwhile, make the cream sauce: In a small bowl, stir together the crema or crème fraîche and yogurt. Season with salt and pepper. Set aside.

3. In a separate small bowl, toss together the mozzarella and Monterey jack cheeses.

4. Preheat the oven to 350°F (180°C). Oil a 2½-qt (2.5-l) baking dish.

5. Spoon half of the rice over the bottom of the prepared dish in an even layer. Cover with half of the tomato sauce and then spread with half of the cream sauce. Scatter half of the cheese mixture evenly over the cream sauce. Repeat the layering, but do not top with the remaining cheese. Lightly cover the baking dish with aluminum foil.

6. Bake until heated through and bubbling along the edges, about 30 minutes. Uncover and sprinkle with the reserved cheese. Return to the oven and continue to bake, uncovered, until the cheese melts, 10–15 minutes. Remove from the oven and let stand for 5 minutes.

7. Spoon the pudding onto individual plates to serve.

SERVES 8–10

NUTRITIONAL ANALYSIS PER SERVING
Calories 404 (Kilojoules 1,670); Protein 11 g; Carbohydrates 31 g; Total Fat 27 g;
Saturated Fat 12 g; Cholesterol 49 mg; Sodium 563 mg; Dietary Fiber 2 g

TOMATO SAUCE

¼ cup (2 fl oz/60 ml) extra-virgin olive oil

1 white onion, slivered

2 cloves garlic, minced

3 large poblano chiles, roasted, peeled, and seeded (page 138), then cut into narrow strips

1 can (15 oz/470 g) plum (Roma) tomatoes with juice, coarsely puréed

1 can (15 oz/470 g) diced tomatoes with juice

½ teaspoon dried Mexican oregano

1 bay leaf

pinch of sugar

kosher salt and freshly ground pepper to taste

CREAM SAUCE

1 cup (8 fl oz/250 ml) crema or crème fraîche

1 cup (8 oz/250 g) plain yogurt

kosher salt and freshly ground pepper to taste

1 cup (4 oz/125 g) shredded mozzarella cheese

1 cup (4 oz/125 g) shredded Monterey jack cheese

3 cups (15 oz/470 g) Seasoned White Rice (page 94)

Grilled Vegetables with Poblano Sauce

VEGETABLES

12 small yellow-fleshed potatoes

1 zucchini (courgette)

2 Asian (slender) eggplants (aubergines)

1 large red bell pepper (capsicum)

1 large yellow bell pepper (capsicum)

1 large red (Spanish) onion

1 large chayote

1 fennel bulb

1–1½ lb (500–750 g) asparagus

olive oil for brushing

kosher salt and freshly ground pepper to taste

POBLANO SAUCE

4 poblano chiles

1 small white onion, cut into slices ½ inch (12 mm) thick

3 cloves garlic, unpeeled

1 small bunch fresh cilantro (fresh coriander)

¼ cup (2 fl oz/60 ml) water

¼ cup (2 fl oz/60 ml) olive or vegetable oil

1–2 tablespoons fresh lime juice

kosher salt to taste

When Southwestern markets and gardens abound with summer produce, I make these spicy vegetables as an accompaniment to grilled meat or poultry.

1. Prepare a fire in a charcoal grill.

2. Prepare all the vegetables for grilling: Bring a saucepan three-fourths full of water to a boil, add the potatoes, parboil for 8–10 minutes, drain, and set aside. Slice the zucchini crosswise ¼ inch (6 mm) thick. Slice the unpeeled eggplants on the diagonal ¼ inch (6 mm) thick. Halve the bell peppers lengthwise, remove the seeds, and cut each half lengthwise into thirds. Cut the onion through the stem end into 8 wedges. Slice the chayote crosswise through the pit ½ inch (12 mm) thick. Trim the fennel bulb and cut lengthwise into 8 wedges. Snap off the tough ends of the asparagus. Brush all the vegetables with olive oil and season with salt and pepper.

3. To make the sauce, grill the chiles, turning as necessary, until evenly blackened and blistered. Remove from the grill, cover loosely with aluminum foil, and let cool for 10 minutes, then peel away the skins and discard the stems and seeds. Grill the onion slices and garlic cloves on a fine-mesh screen, turning once, until lightly golden, 6–8 minutes total. Remove from the grill and peel the garlic cloves. In a blender, combine the chiles, onion slices, garlic, cilantro, water, and oil and purée until smooth. Stir in the lime juice and kosher salt. Set aside.

4. Place the prepared vegetables on the grill rack and grill, turning as necessary, until tender and nicely charred: 4–5 minutes for the potatoes; 4–6 minutes for the zucchini and eggplants; 6–7 minutes for the bell peppers; about 8 minutes for the onion wedges, chayote, and fennel; and 4–5 minutes for the asparagus.

5. Divide the vegetables among individual plates and drizzle with the sauce, or serve it alongside in small bowls.

SERVES 6

NUTRITIONAL ANALYSIS PER SERVING
Calories 361 (Kilojoules 1,516); Protein 9 g; Carbohydrates 44 g; Total Fat 19 g; Saturated Fat 2 g; Cholesterol 0 mg; Sodium 130 mg; Dietary Fiber 7 g

Ranch Baked Beans

2½ cups (17½ oz/545 g) dried pinto beans

1 ham hock, cut into thirds crosswise

1 medium-sized white onion, chopped, plus 1 large onion, finely chopped

3 cloves garlic, minced, plus 2 large cloves garlic, minced

¼ teaspoon ground allspice

2½ teaspoons plus 1 tablespoon dried Mexican oregano

1 tablespoon chile caribe

2 bay leaves

2 canela sticks or cinnamon sticks

3 teaspoons each cumin and coriander seed, toasted and ground (page 141)

3½ qt (3.5 l) water, or as needed

1 cup (6 oz/185 g) canned diced tomatoes

2 tablespoons tomato paste

2 teaspoons kosher salt

½ cup (4 fl oz/125 ml) chili sauce

⅓ cup (2½ oz/75 g) firmly packed brown sugar

¼ cup (2 fl oz/60 ml) Worcestershire sauce

3 tablespoons yellow mustard

1 teaspoon freshly ground canela or ¾ teaspoon ground cinnamon

½ teaspoon freshly ground pepper

⅛ teaspoon ground cloves

6 oz (185 g) chilled bacon, julienned

6 tablespoons (3 fl oz/90 ml) gold tequila

1. Pick over the beans, discarding any stones, and rinse well. Place in a bowl with water to cover by 2 inches (5 cm) and let stand overnight. The next day, drain the beans and place in a large pot along with the ham hock, medium-sized onion, 3 minced garlic cloves, allspice, the 2½ teaspoons oregano, chile caribe, bay leaves, canela or cinnamon sticks, two-thirds of the cumin and coriander, and the 3½ qt (3.5 l) water. Bring to a boil, reduce the heat to low, cover, and simmer until the beans are nearly tender but still quite firm, about 1 hour. Uncover the pot, stir in the tomatoes, tomato paste, and salt, and continue to simmer, uncovered, until the beans are much softer but still hold their shape and the liquid has reduced, about 1 hour, adding more water if needed to prevent sticking.

2. Preheat the oven to 350°F (180°C).

3. Remove the ham hock, bay leaves, and canela or cinnamon sticks and discard. Scrape the beans into a large bowl and stir in the chili sauce, brown sugar, Worcestershire sauce, mustard, the remaining 1 tablespoon oregano, the remaining ground cumin and coriander, the ground canela or cinnamon, the pepper, and the cloves. In a frying pan over medium-high heat, fry the bacon until it renders some of its fat, 3–4 minutes. Add the finely chopped onion and cook, stirring often, until the onion is soft, about 5 minutes. Add the 2 minced garlic cloves and cook for 1 minute. Pour in the tequila, stir well, and cook for 1 minute longer.

4. Pour the contents of the frying pan into the beans and mix well. Then pour the bean mixture into an ungreased 3-qt (3-l) baking dish. Place in the oven and bake until bubbly and the top is lightly browned, 50–55 minutes.

5. Remove the beans from the oven and let stand for 5 minutes, then serve directly from the dish.

SERVES 8–10

NUTRITIONAL ANALYSIS PER SERVING
Calories 421 (Kilojoules 1,768); Protein 19 g; Carbohydrates 57 g; Total Fat 14 g; Saturated Fat 5 g; Cholesterol 23 mg; Sodium 1,129 mg; Dietary Fiber 8 g

In 1821, when Mexico achieved independence from Spain, New Mexico came under Mexican rule and trade was opened with the United States. The Santa Fe Trail became the link, carrying wagon trains of new people and supplies from the Midwest and the East to the Southwest.

Starting in Independence, Missouri, the trail provided the shortest diagonal route to the Southwest. It split into two branches in Kansas, north through the mountains and south through the harsh heat. A little north of Santa Fe the branches reunited, and the trail ended in the heart of the town.

Trappers, frontiersmen, and traders traveled this road, carrying with them new cooking utensils and foodstuffs, and opened the territory for settlement. By the 1840s, stagecoaches were regularly traveling between St. Louis and Santa Fe, and for the next thirty years, until the completion of the railroad, the trail remained the economic lifeline to the Southwest.

A melting pot of nationalities—English, Irish, French, German, Polish, Norwegian, Swedish—arrived by way of the trail. They carried recipes, cooking techniques, and equipment,

Santa Fe **Trail**

but because pioneers are more likely to eat whatever their new home offers, these outsiders soon adapted their habits to Southwest ingredients. Of course, some ingredients and ideas made their way east along the trail, too, but it would take until the latter part of the twentieth century before Southwest dishes would gain popularity elsewhere in the country.

Spring Vegetable Ragout with Herbs

2 teaspoons safflower oil

1 small head garlic, halved lengthwise

2 leeks, including 2 inches (5 cm)
of pale green, cut into 1-inch
(2.5-cm) pieces

2 carrots, peeled and coarsely chopped

tender leaves and small tender stalks
from 1 bunch celery, cut up

2 zucchini (courgettes), cut up

2 red bell peppers (capsicums), seeded
and coarsely chopped

12 snow peas (mangetouts), cut up

8 fresh flat-leaf (Italian) parsley sprigs

1 bunch fresh cilantro (fresh coriander),
coarsely chopped

1 tablespoon kosher salt

6 cups (48 fl oz/1.5 l) water

12 baby carrots, unpeeled and tops
trimmed to ¼ inch (6 mm)

1 bunch French breakfast radishes,
trimmed but left whole

6 small white Japanese turnips, stems
trimmed and quartered lengthwise

1 lb (500 g) young, tender fava (broad)
beans, shelled

1 lb (500 g) English peas, shelled

½ lb (250 g) haricots verts, trimmed

24 cherry tomatoes, stems removed

2 teaspoons each chopped fresh
tarragon and dill

1 tablespoon snipped fresh chives

6 fresh chervil sprigs

Southwestern farmers and gardeners have succumbed to the widespread passion for baby vegetables and such previously hard-to-find produce as French radishes, fava beans, and haricots verts. I love combining them in this delightful mélange, which I serve on its own as a vegetarian main course or as a starter to precede roast meats, poultry, or seafood.

1. To make the stock, in a large saucepan over medium-high heat, warm the safflower oil. Add the garlic, leeks, chopped carrots, celery leaves and stalks, zucchini, bell peppers, snow peas, parsley, and cilantro. Cook, stirring frequently, until the vegetables are soft, about 10 minutes. Add the salt and water and bring to a boil over high heat. Reduce the heat to low and simmer, uncovered, for 45 minutes. Strain immediately through a fine-mesh sieve. Discard the contents of the sieve.

2. Pour the stock into a dutch oven and bring to a boil over high heat. Add the baby carrots, radishes, and turnips and cook for 5 minutes. Add the fava beans, peas, and haricots verts and continue to cook until all the vegetables are just tender, 3–4 minutes. Using a slotted spoon, transfer the vegetables to a bowl; keep warm. Raise the heat to high and reduce the cooking liquid to 3 cups (24 fl oz/750 ml), 10–12 minutes.

3. Divide the cooked vegetables and the cherry tomatoes evenly among shallow individual soup bowls. Sprinkle evenly with the tarragon, dill, and chives. Add ½ cup (4 fl oz/125 ml) of the reduced stock to each of the bowls. Serve immediately, topped with the chervil sprigs.

SERVES 6

NUTRITIONAL ANALYSIS PER SERVING
Calories 183 (Kilojoules 769); Protein 8 g; Carbohydrates 37 g; Total Fat 3 g;
Saturated Fat 0 g; Cholesterol 0 mg; Sodium 933 mg; Dietary Fiber 10 g

Three-Bean Ragout with Rajas

½ cup (3½ oz/105 g) dried black runner beans

½ cup (3½ oz/105 g) dried Anasazi beans

½ cup (3½ oz/105 g) dried pinto beans

6 tablespoons (3 fl oz/90 ml) extra-virgin olive oil

3 tablespoons white wine vinegar

½ teaspoon dried Mexican oregano

pinch of sugar

kosher salt and freshly ground pepper to taste

3 tablespoons olive oil

1 small white onion, slivered

1 large clove garlic, coarsely chopped

2 poblano chiles, roasted, peeled, and seeded *(page 138),* then cut into narrow strips 1 inch (2.5 cm) long

1 large red bell pepper (capsicum), roasted, peeled, and seeded *(page 138),* then cut into narrow strips 1 inch (2.5 cm) long

1 large yellow bell pepper (capsicum), roasted, peeled, and seeded *(page 138),* then cut into narrow strips 1 inch (2.5 cm) long

Rajas, Spanish for "strips," are slices of roasted chiles, and are often combined with grilled or sautéed onions and garlic. Serve the ragout alongside grilled or roasted meats, spoon it over rice, or toss it with pasta.

1. First, prepare the beans: Keeping the black, Anasazi, and pinto beans separate, pick them over, discarding any misshapen beans or stones. Rinse well, then soak overnight in water to cover. Drain the beans and place each variety in a separate small saucepan. Add water to cover generously, bring to a boil, reduce the heat to simmer, and cook until tender, about 1 hour.

2. In a large bowl, whisk together the extra-virgin olive oil, vinegar, oregano, sugar, salt, and pepper to make a dressing. When the beans are ready, drain them and add to the dressing while the beans are still warm. Toss well. Set the beans aside, stirring them every so often while you finish the recipe.

3. In a large frying pan over medium-high heat, warm the oil. Add the onion and sauté until softened, about 3 minutes. Add the garlic and cook for 1 minute longer. Add the chile strips, bell pepper strips, and beans, reduce the heat to low, and cook, stirring, until all the ingredients are heated through, just a few minutes. Season the ragout with salt and pepper and transfer to a warmed bowl. Serve immediately.

SERVES 8

NUTRITIONAL ANALYSIS PER SERVING
Calories 283 (Kilojoules 1,189); Protein 9 g; Carbohydrates 28 g; Total Fat 16 g; Saturated Fat 2 g; Cholesterol 0 mg; Sodium 7 mg; Dietary Fiber 5 g

Red Chile–Charred Tomato Salsa

4 dried New Mexico red chiles, seeded

2 morita chiles

4 large, ripe plum (Roma) tomatoes

3 large cloves garlic, unpeeled

1 small white onion, cut into slices
    ½ inch (12 mm) thick

½ teaspoon dried Mexican oregano

pinch of sugar

kosher salt to taste

1 tablespoon orange-flavored olive oil

1. Place all the chiles in a frying pan over medium-high heat and press with a kitchen towel for 2–3 seconds. Flip and press again for 2–3 seconds. Immerse fully in a bowl of hot water for about 20 minutes. Drain, reserving the water, and place the chiles in a blender with ¼ cup (2 fl oz/ 60 ml) of the water. Purée until the consistency of heavy (double) cream, adding more water if necessary. Pour through a medium-mesh sieve and set aside.

2. Place the tomatoes in a cast-iron frying pan over medium-high heat and char on all sides. Set aside to cool. Char the garlic cloves and the onion slices in the same way and let cool. Peel the tomatoes and place in a food processor. Peel and mince the garlic, and cut up the onion slices. Add to the processor and pulse until the tomatoes are coarsely chopped. Add the chile purée, oregano, sugar, and salt.

3. Pour into a bowl and drizzle with the oil. Let stand for 20 minutes before serving. The salsa will keep well covered and refrigerated for 2–3 days.

MAKES 2½ CUPS (20 FL OZ/625 ML)

Fresh Tomato Salsa

The yellow, red, and orange of the tomatoes create an attractively colorful salad. If you like, substitute yellow and red baby plum tomatoes as suggested on page 80, or try your own combination.

In a bowl, combine all the cherry tomatoes, the onion, chives, cilantro, mint, and chiles. Stir gently to combine. Add the vinegar, lime-flavored oil, sugar, and salt and toss to mix. Let the mixture stand for 10 minutes. Taste and adjust the seasoning. Serve immediately.

MAKES ABOUT 2½ CUPS (20 FL OZ/625 ML)

¾ cup (4½ oz/140 g) each yellow, red, and orange cherry tomatoes, stems removed and halved lengthwise

1 small red (Spanish) onion, finely diced

1 tablespoon snipped fresh chives

1 tablespoon chopped fresh cilantro (fresh coriander)

2 teaspoons chopped fresh mint

2 serrano chiles, minced

2 tablespoons white wine vinegar

1–2 tablespoons lime-flavored olive oil

pinch of sugar

kosher salt to taste

Pan-Seared Tomatillo Salsa

1 lb (500 g) tomatillos (about 12)

2 or 3 cloves garlic

2 small spring onions or small white onions

4 or 5 serrano chiles, stems removed

⅓–½ cup (3–4 fl oz/80–125 ml) water

1 bunch fresh cilantro (fresh coriander), coarsely chopped

zest of 1 lime

pinch of sugar

kosher salt to taste

2–3 tablespoons lime-flavored olive oil

The tart taste of the tomatillo, which resembles but is unrelated to green tomatoes, makes this salsa especially refreshing with seafood or poultry.

1. In a bowl, combine the tomatillos with warm water to cover and let stand for 5 minutes to remove any sticky residue on the skins. Drain, remove the husks, and rinse the tomatillos.

2. Place a cast-iron frying pan over high heat. Add the tomatillos, garlic, onions, and chiles and char them on all sides, turning them as needed. Transfer the contents of the pan to a food processor. Let the ingredients cool for 10 minutes.

3. Pulse the tomatillo mixture until reduced to a coarse purée. Transfer to a bowl and thin to the desired consistency with water. Stir in the cilantro, lime zest, sugar, salt, and olive oil to taste. Let stand for 20 minutes for the flavors to meld before serving. The salsa will keep well covered and refrigerated for 1 day.

MAKES ABOUT 2½ CUPS (20 FL OZ/625 ML)

Tomatillo-Avocado Salsa

1 lb (500 g) tomatillos (about 12)

1 large, ripe Haas avocado, pitted, peeled, and cut into ½-inch (12-mm) cubes

1 small white onion, finely diced

2 cloves garlic, finely chopped

3 serrano chiles, finely chopped

fresh lime juice to taste

pinch of sugar

kosher salt to taste

2 tablespoons olive oil

¼ cup (⅓ oz/10 g) coarsely chopped fresh cilantro (fresh coriander)

1. In a bowl, combine the tomatillos with warm water to cover and let stand for 5 minutes to remove any sticky residue on the skins. Drain, remove the husks, then rinse and quarter the tomatillos.

2. Place the tomatillos in a food processor and pulse until coarsely puréed. Pour into a bowl and gently stir in the avocado cubes. Add the onion, garlic, and chiles and mix well. Season with the lime juice, sugar, and salt, then stir in the olive oil and cilantro. If the mixture seems too thick, add water to thin to the desired consistency.

3. Let stand for 20 minutes to meld the flavors before serving. The salsa will keep well covered and refrigerated for 2 days.

MAKES ABOUT 3 CUPS (24 FL OZ/750 ML)

4 Desserts & Beverages

Southwestern food is typically hot and spicy, so cool, refreshing fruit often caps off the meal. More elaborate finales have been borrowed from Spanish and Mexican traditions, such as *bizcochitos, capirotada,* and flan, but each has been given a distinctly Southwestern character through flavoring or technique. Many contemporary beverages owe their origins to these same influences, from the hot chocolate adapted from an early Mexican recipe to the cold, colorful, fruit-laced, Spanish-inspired sangria that locals slowly sip on summer's hottest days. Adaptation even reaches to the British Isles, with the use of the region's indigenous piñon nuts in the Southwestern version of shortbread brought by the Scottish settlers.

Fresh Fruits in Prickly Pear Syrup

SYRUP

2½ lb (1.25 kg) prickly pears (14–16
  fruits), or 2 cups (16 fl oz/500 ml)
  unsweetened prickly pear juice

½ cup (4 fl oz/125 ml) water

1 cup (8 oz/250 g) sugar

1 bunch fresh mint

1 canela or cinnamon stick

1 vanilla bean, split lengthwise

FRUIT

1 large, ripe mango

1 small, ripe pineapple, peeled, halved
  lengthwise, core removed, and cut
  into ½-inch (12-mm) cubes

6 large strawberries, stems removed
  and quartered lengthwise

1 cup (4 oz/125 g) blueberries

1 cup (4 oz/125 g) blackberries

1 cup (4 oz/125 g) raspberries

6 fresh mint sprigs

Known in Spanish as *tuna,* the fruit of the prickly pear cactus
has juicy flesh and a flavor reminiscent of watermelon. If
you cannot find the fresh fruits, cans of the prepared juice
can be bought in specialty-food stores.

1. First, make the syrup: If using the fresh prickly pears, working with
1 fruit at a time, and using the tip of a sharp knife, scrape off the thorny
nodes. Trim off the ends of the fruit, make a lengthwise slit through the
skin, and peel off and discard the skin. Repeat with the remaining fruits.
Cut the fruits into large pieces, transfer to a food processor, and process
until puréed, 10–12 seconds. Strain through a medium-mesh sieve. You
should have 2 cups (16 fl oz/500 ml).

2. In a saucepan, combine the prickly pear purée or juice, water, sugar,
mint, and canela or cinnamon stick. Scrape the seeds from the vanilla
bean into the pan, then add the pod halves. Bring to a boil over medium-
high heat, stirring to dissolve the sugar. Reduce the heat to medium-low
and simmer, uncovered, for 20 minutes. Taste and make sure the flavors
are balanced. Strain through a fine-mesh sieve.

3. Cut the flesh of the mango away from the seed in 2 large slices, then
score the flesh of each slice in ½-inch (12-mm) cubes, cutting to the skin.
Holding a mango slice over another bowl, invert the skin and cut the
cubes away, letting them fall into the bowl. Repeat with the other slice.
Add the pineapple to the bowl and mix gently to combine.

4. Place a spoonful of the mixture in each of 6 small glass bowls or
martini glasses. Divide the strawberries, blueberries, blackberries, and
raspberries among the glasses or bowls. Ladle the syrup over the fruits,
garnish with mint, and serve.

SERVES 6

NUTRITIONAL ANALYSIS PER SERVING
Calories 337 (Kilojoules 1,415); Protein 3 g; Carbohydrates 84 g; Total Fat 2 g;
Saturated Fat 0 g; Cholesterol 0 mg; Sodium 14 mg; Dietary Fiber 10 g

Toasted Piñon Shortbread

2 cups (10 oz/315 g) unbleached all-purpose (plain) flour

½ cup (4 oz/125 g) sugar

½ cup (2½ oz/75 g) piñon nuts or other pine nuts

2 teaspoons freshly ground canela or 1½ teaspoons ground cinnamon

pinch of kosher salt

1 cup (8 oz/250 g) chilled unsalted butter, cut into tablespoon-sized pieces

The piñon pine *(Pinus edulis)* grows profusely on the public lands of New Mexico, Arizona, and Colorado. Extracted from its cones, the plump nuts, called piñons, have a richer and more resinous flavor than that of imported pine nuts from the Mediterranean and are about half their size. They are enjoyed in all manner of sweets, including these simple, buttery cookies.

1. Preheat the oven to 300°F (150°C). Line a baking sheet with parchment (baking) paper.

2. In a food processor, combine the flour, sugar, nuts, canela or cinnamon, and salt. Pulse 10 times to combine the ingredients and to coarsely chop the nuts. Add the butter and process until the mixture just comes together into a ball. (The dough may be wrapped and refrigerated at this point for up to 2 days.)

3. On a lightly floured work surface, roll out the dough about ½ inch (12 mm) thick. Using a 2-inch (5-cm) round cookie cutter, cut out the cookies. Gather the scraps, reroll, and cut out more cookies until the dough is used up. Place the cutouts on the baking sheet. Slip the baking sheet into the refrigerator or freezer to chill for 1 hour. (The cookies may be frozen at this point on the tray, then transferred to a lock-top plastic bag; they will keep frozen for up to 1 month.)

4. Bake the shortbread cookies, in batches, until slightly puffed and firm but not browned, about 45 minutes. Transfer the baking sheet to a rack and let cool for 10 minutes, then transfer the cookies to the rack and let cool completely.

MAKES ABOUT 30 COOKIES

NUTRITIONAL ANALYSIS PER COOKIE
Calories 118 (Kilojoules 496); Protein 2 g; Carbohydrates 12 g; Total Fat 7 g; Saturated Fat 4 g; Cholesterol 17 mg; Sodium 4 mg; Dietary Fiber 1 g

Bizcochitos

1 cup (8 oz/250 g) lard or vegetable shortening, at room temperature

½ cup (4 oz/125 g) sugar, plus ⅓ cup (3 oz/90 g) sugar mixed with 1 teaspoon freshly ground canela or ¾ teaspoon ground cinnamon

pinch of kosher salt

1 egg

3 cups (15 oz/470 g) unbleached all-purpose (plain) flour

2 teaspoons baking powder

2 teaspoons aniseed, toasted *(page 141)*

2 tablespoons dark rum or brandy

The traditional Christmas cookies of New Mexico gain their licorice flavor from aniseed, introduced to the region by the Spanish in the early nineteenth century. The classic shape for this crumbly delicacy is the fleur-de-lys, but round is also common.

1. Preheat the oven to 350°F (180°C). Line 3 baking sheets with parchment (baking) paper. In a bowl, using an electric mixer set on medium-high speed, beat together the lard or shortening and ½ cup (4 oz/125 g) sugar until light and fluffy. Add the salt and egg, reduce the speed to low, and mix until combined.

2. In a separate bowl, whisk together the flour, baking powder, and aniseed. With the mixer on low speed, add the flour mixture to the lard or shortening mixture and beat until just combined. Add the rum or brandy and mix until combined. If the dough still seems too dry to hold together, add water, 1 teaspoon at a time, until the dough comes together.

3. On a lightly floured work surface, roll out the dough about ¼ inch (6 mm) thick. Using a 2-inch (5-cm) cookie cutter, cut out the cookies. Gather the scraps, reroll, and cut out more cookies until the dough is used up. Place the cookies on the prepared baking sheets. Sprinkle with the canela-sugar mixture.

4. Bake the cookies, one baking sheet at a time, until puffed and very lightly golden, about 12 minutes. Remove from the oven and let the cookies cool on the baking sheets for 5 minutes. Transfer the cookies to racks to cool completely. Repeat with the remaining cookies. The cookies will keep for 3–4 days in a cool, dry place, such as an airtight tin, between layers of parchment or waxed paper.

MAKES ABOUT 45 COOKIES

NUTRITIONAL ANALYSIS PER COOKIE
Calories 102 (Kilojoules 428); Protein 1 g; Carbohydrates 12 g; Total Fat 5 g; Saturated Fat 2 g; Cholesterol 10 mg; Sodium 26 mg; Dietary Fiber 0 g

In the scenic foothills of the Sangre de Cristo Mountains, just northwest of Santa Fe, lies the community of Chimayó. Its original settlers arrived before the English founded Jamestown, Virginia, and by the eighteenth century, the village, named by Tewa Indians for the area's flaking red rock, had evolved into a close-knit community of small farms.

In order to survive, neighboring families shared grazing lands, irrigation ditches, and labor. Hardworking and self-sufficient, these farmers grew the same crops the Pueblo Indians had grown for centuries: corn, beans, squash, and chiles, bolstered by wheat, tree fruits, grapes, and melons. Imported products such as coffee, sugar, and spices remained scarce.

Today, visitors come to Chimayó for its superior red chiles, which are dried and strung into *ristras* in the fall, and to see the town's lovely centuries-old church, the Santuario de Chimayó. They are also drawn by the restaurant and inn known as Rancho de Chimayó. The latter is housed in the restored homes of the brothers Hermenegildo and Epifanio Jaramillo, whose ancestors arrived in the area in 1680. The whitewashed walls, the hand-stripped *vigas* (beams), and

Chimayó

the terraced patios provide an Old World haven. Arturo, who opened the operation in the 1960s, wanted a restaurant where diners would feel like guests in an old Spanish home and would be able to feast on the very best traditional dishes the region has to offer. Many Southwesterners will tell you that he has succeeded in doing just that.

Tres Leches Flan

1 can (12 fl oz/375 ml) evaporated milk

1 can (14 fl oz/440 ml) sweetened condensed milk

1 cup (8 fl oz/250 ml) heavy (double) cream

pinch of kosher salt

½ teaspoon freshly ground canela or ¼ teaspoon ground cinnamon

1 tablespoon Grand Marnier, Cointreau, or other orange-flavored liqueur

1 tablespoon vanilla extract (essence)

⅔ cup (5 oz/155 g) sugar

2 whole eggs plus 6 egg yolks

Typically, the *tres leches*—"three milks"—combination is used to make celebratory cakes in Mexico, particularly in the northwestern coastal state of Sinaloa, across the border from the American Southwest. That proximity explains the use of the same trio to make this thick, creamy custard.

1. In a saucepan, combine the evaporated milk, sweetened condensed milk, cream, salt, canela or cinnamon, liqueur, and vanilla and bring just to a boil. Remove from the heat and set aside to cool.

2. In a small, heavy frying pan over medium-high heat, melt the sugar, without stirring, until it becomes a clear amber syrup, 6–8 minutes. Pour it quickly into a 9½-inch (24-cm) ring mold (5-cup/40–fl oz/1.25-l capacity). Holding the mold with potholders, carefully and quickly rotate it to spread the caramelized sugar over the bottom and up the sides, coating evenly. Set aside to cool and set.

3. Position a rack in the lower third of the oven and preheat the oven to 325°F (165°C).

4. In a small bowl, whisk together the whole eggs and yolks, and then whisk them into the steeped milk mixture. Pour into the caramel-lined ring mold. Place the mold in a baking pan. Pour hot water into the baking pan to reach three-fourths of the way up the sides of the mold.

5. Bake until the custard is set but still jiggles in the center, about 40 minutes. Transfer the mold to a rack and let cool completely.

6. To unmold, run a thin knife blade around the inside edge of the mold and invert onto a serving plate. The caramel will run down over the edges. Cut into 8–10 portions, transfer to individual plates, and spoon a little of the caramel over each serving.

SERVES 8–10

NUTRITIONAL ANALYSIS PER SERVING
Calories 413 (Kilojoules 1,735); Protein 10 g; Carbohydrates 46 g; Total Fat 21 g; Saturated Fat 12 g; Cholesterol 252 mg; Sodium 139 mg; Dietary Fiber 0 g

Chocolate-Pecan Torte

6 oz (185 g) bittersweet chocolate, chopped into small pieces

2 cups (8 oz/250 g) ground pecans

3 tablespoons unbleached all-purpose (plain) flour

pinch of kosher salt

¾ cup (6 oz/185 g) unsalted butter, at room temperature

½ cup (4 oz/125 g) plus 2 tablespoons sugar

6 eggs, separated

FROSTING

1 cup (8 fl oz/250 ml) heavy (double) cream

¼ cup (2 fl oz/60 ml) hot water

2 tablespoons sugar

1½ tablespoons instant espresso powder

4 oz (125 g) bittersweet chocolate, chopped into small pieces

2 egg yolks

pecan halves

Chocolate desserts in the Southwest are typically intense in flavor and dense in texture, like this pecan-rich torte.

1. Preheat the oven to 350°F (180°C). Butter a 9½-inch (24-cm) round cake pan. Line the bottom with parchment (baking) paper.

2. In a small saucepan over low heat, melt the chocolate and stir until smooth. Set aside. In a small bowl, combine the ground pecans, flour, and salt. In a separate bowl, using an electric mixer set on medium-high speed, beat together the butter and the ½ cup (4 oz/125 g) sugar until fluffy. Add the egg yolks, one at a time, beating well after each addition. Stir in the melted chocolate and the pecan mixture.

3. In a bowl, whisk the egg whites with the 2 tablespoons sugar until they hold soft peaks. Pour into the chocolate mixture and gently but thoroughly combine the two. Pour into the prepared pan and smooth the top.

4. Bake until a toothpick inserted into the center comes out clean, about 45 minutes. Transfer to a rack and let cool for 10 minutes, then invert onto a plate, peel off the parchment, and invert onto the rack to cool completely.

5. To make the frosting, in a bowl, whisk the cream until soft peaks form. Cover and set aside. In a small bowl, combine the hot water, sugar, and espresso and stir to dissolve the espresso and sugar. In a small saucepan over low heat, melt the chocolate and stir until smooth. Stir in the espresso mixture and then the egg yolks until smooth. Add to the whipped cream, combining thoroughly. Cover and refrigerate until firm enough to frost the torte, about 1 hour.

6. Place the torte on a plate and frost the top and sides thickly. Decorate the top edge with the pecan halves. Chill before serving.

SERVES 8–10

NUTRITIONAL ANALYSIS PER SERVING
Calories 690 (Kilojoules 2,898); Protein 10 g; Carbohydrates 42 g; Total Fat 58 g;
Saturated Fat 24 g; Cholesterol 268 mg; Sodium 76 mg; Dietary Fiber 2 g

Apple-Pecan Crisp

TOPPING

⅓ cup (3 oz/90 g) firmly packed light brown sugar

¾ cup (4 oz/125 g) unbleached all-purpose (plain) flour

pinch of kosher salt

1 teaspoon minced lemon or orange zest

6 tablespoons (3 oz/90 g) chilled unsalted butter, cut into pieces

1½ lb (750 g) Granny Smith apples, halved, cored, peeled, and cut lengthwise into slices ¼ inch (6 mm) thick

1½ lb (750 g) McIntosh apples, halved, cored, peeled, and cut lengthwise into slices ¼ inch (6 mm) thick

2 tablespoons tapioca starch

3 tablespoons fresh lemon juice

1 tablespoon minced lemon zest

2 tablespoons unsalted butter, cut into small pieces

½ cup (2 oz/60 g) coarsely chopped pecans

½ cup (4 fl oz/125 ml) crema or crème fraîche

Spanish settlers introduced a wide variety of fruit trees to the Southwest including apple trees, which now flourish in northern New Mexico. Pecan trees, native to the Southwest, proliferate in Texas and New Mexico, the nation's second and third largest producers of the nut, respectively.

1. Preheat the oven to 350°F (180°C). Butter a 2-qt (2-l) baking dish.

2. To make the topping, in a food processor, combine the brown sugar, flour, salt, and citrus zest and pulse several times to combine thoroughly. Add the butter and process to the consistency of coarse meal. Set aside. (This mixture can be covered and refrigerated or frozen for up to 2 weeks.)

3. In a large bowl, combine the apple slices, tapioca starch, lemon juice, and lemon zest. Transfer to the prepared baking dish. Dot evenly with the butter pieces, then strew ¼ cup (1 oz/30 g) of the pecans evenly over the top. Sprinkle the topping in an even layer over the apples, and finally top with the remaining ¼ cup (1 oz/30 g) pecans.

4. Bake until the top is browned and the filling is bubbly, about 40 minutes. Serve warm or at room temperature, scooping servings into individual bowls. Top each serving with some crema or crème fraîche.

SERVES 6–8

NUTRITIONAL ANALYSIS PER SERVING
Calories 450 (Kilojoules 1,890); Protein 3 g; Carbohydrates 54 g; Total Fat 26 g; Saturated Fat 13 g; Cholesterol 51 mg; Sodium 51 mg; Dietary Fiber 4 g

Long ago, the wild nuts and seeds of the Southwest were primary contributors of flavor, texture, dense calories, and oils to the diet of the Native Americans. Today's Southwest cooks turn out a tableful of distinctive regional dishes that draw upon many of the same nuts and seeds, as well as others.

Piñon, or pine, nuts grow on native dwarf pines, are harvested only by hand, and rarely leave the region. These plump white kernels, which are actually seeds, are added to salads, soups, sauces, and desserts such as shortbread.

Pepitas, or pumpkin seeds, have been eaten by natives of the Southwest for centuries. Today, they are dried and toasted and then often salted for a snack. Unsalted, they are ground to thicken sauces or left whole for adding to salads.

Pecans, members of the walnut family and native to the Americas, are sweet, rich, crunchy nuts. In the past, Native Americans used liquid extracted from them in the making of corn cakes. Nowadays, the nuts add flavor and texture to savory and sweet dishes and especially to the chocolate desserts of the modern Southwest table.

Nuts and Seeds

Pistachios, which are native to the Levant, have been embraced by Southwest cooks, and drought-resistant pistachio trees are now grown in this semiarid region. The nuts are often eaten out of hand, but they can also show up in modern versions of old Southwest favorites, such as the homey bread pudding known as *capirotada.*

Capirotada with Pistachios and Dried Fruits

6 cups (12 oz/375 g) cubed day-old Italian or French bread (¾–1-inch/2–2.5-cm cubes)

1 cup (8 fl oz/250 ml) gold tequila or sweet wine such as Marsala

⅓ cup (2 oz/60 g) dried currants

½ cup (2 oz/60 g) dried sour cherries

½ cup (3 oz/90 g) diced dried apricots

1½ cups (12 oz/375 g) sugar

2½ cups (20 fl oz/625 ml) water

¼ cup (2 oz/60 g) unsalted butter

1 vanilla bean, split lengthwise

1 canela or cinnamon stick

¼ teaspoon freshly grated nutmeg

pinch of ground allspice

¾ cup (3 oz/90 g) pistachios, piñon nuts, or pecans, toasted

1 cup (4 oz/125 g) shredded Monterey jack cheese

1 cup (4 oz/125 g) shredded mild cheddar cheese

½ cup (4 fl oz/125 ml) crema or crème fraîche

This typical bread pudding of the old Southwest substitutes cheese for the more familiar milk and eggs in such recipes. Pistachios, which are cultivated in New Mexico, Arizona, and west Texas, add a delightful crunch.

1. Preheat the oven to 350°F (180°C). Butter a 2-qt (2-l) baking dish.

2. Spread the bread cubes on a baking sheet and toast in the oven, turning to brown evenly, until lightly golden, 8–10 minutes. Set aside.

3. In a small saucepan over medium heat, combine the tequila or wine, currants, and sour cherries. Bring the mixture to a boil, reduce the heat to low, and simmer for 3 minutes. Remove from the heat and let stand for 10 minutes. Stir in the apricots and set aside.

4. In a heavy saucepan over medium-high heat, warm the sugar until it begins to melt around the edges of the pan. Then begin to mash it gently with a spoon, but do not stir. Continue to cook the sugar until it starts to turn deep amber, making sure that all of it is melted and it is clear. Immediately add the water in a slow, steady stream, being careful, as it will splatter. The caramel will harden, but then it will remelt as it heats through. When it is again liquid, add the butter, vanilla bean, canela or cinnamon, nutmeg, and allspice and simmer, stirring occasionally, for 10 minutes. Remove from the heat and let stand for 15 minutes. Pour through a fine-mesh sieve placed over a bowl.

5. Layer half of the bread cubes in the prepared baking dish. Sprinkle with half of the fruit mixture and any liquid left in the pan. Sprinkle with half of the nuts and half of the cheeses, and drizzle with half of the syrup. Repeat the layers. Bake until lightly browned and bubbly, about 25 minutes. Spoon into individual bowls and top with the crema or crème fraîche. Serve immediately.

SERVES 8

NUTRITIONAL ANALYSIS PER SERVING
Calories 709 (Kilojoules 2,978); Protein 14 g; Carbohydrates 85 g; Total Fat 28 g; Saturated Fat 14 g; Cholesterol 59 mg; Sodium 426 mg; Dietary Fiber 4 g

Sopaipillas with Canela-Vanilla Ice Cream

ICE CREAM

2 cups (16 fl oz/500 ml) heavy (double) cream

2 cups (16 fl oz/500 ml) milk

1 vanilla bean, split lengthwise

2 canela or cinnamon sticks

pinch of kosher salt

¾ cup (6 oz/185 g) sugar

8 egg yolks

SOPAIPILLAS

¾ cup (4 oz/125 g) unbleached all-purpose (plain) flour

¼ cup (1½ oz/45 g) *panocha* flour or whole-wheat (wholemeal) flour

½ teaspoon kosher salt

½ teaspoon baking powder

1 tablespoon sugar

1 tablespoon lard or vegetable shortening, at room temperature

¼–⅓ cup (2–3 fl oz/60–80 ml) buttermilk

canola oil for deep frying

1. To make the ice cream, pour the cream and milk into a saucepan. Scrape the seeds from the vanilla bean into the pan, then add the pod halves. Add the canela or cinnamon and salt and bring just to a boil. Cover and set aside for 30 minutes.

2. Remove the vanilla bean pods and canela or cinnamon and discard. Add ½ cup (4 oz/125 g) of the sugar and bring to a simmer over medium heat, stirring to dissolve the sugar. In a bowl, whisk together the remaining ¼ cup (2 oz/60 g) sugar with the egg yolks. Slowly whisk 1 cup (8 fl oz/250 ml) of the hot cream mixture into the egg mixture. Then slowly return it to the saucepan, whisking constantly. Cook over low heat, stirring constantly, until thick enough to coat a spoon, 8–10 minutes. Pour through a fine-mesh sieve, let cool, cover, and chill well.

3. Transfer the custard to an ice-cream maker and process according to the manufacturer's instructions. Freeze until serving.

4. To make the sopaipillas, in a food processor, pulse together the flours, salt, baking powder, and sugar. Add the lard or shortening and pulse to combine. Add the buttermilk and pulse until a moist dough forms. Transfer to a lightly floured work surface, and knead several times until it binds into a cohesive mass. Cover with plastic wrap and let rest for 30 minutes.

5. Pour oil to a depth of 4 inches (10 cm) into a heavy saucepan and heat to 375°F (190°C). Meanwhile, divide the dough in half. On a lightly floured work surface, roll out half of the dough ⅛–¼ inch (3–6 mm) thick. Cut into 6 squares or triangles. Drop 2 cutouts, one at a time, into the hot oil and fry, rolling them over, until golden, 40–50 seconds. Drain on paper towels. Repeat with the remaining dough.

6. Serve at once on warmed individual plates with scoops of the ice cream.

SERVES 6

NUTRITIONAL ANALYSIS PER SERVING
Calories 723 (Kilojoules 3,037); Protein 11 g; Carbohydrates 58 g; Total Fat 50 g; Saturated Fat 24 g; Cholesterol 408 mg; Sodium 325 mg; Dietary Fiber 1 g

Watermelon Agua Fresca

8 cups (3 lb/1.5 kg) peeled, seeded and cubed watermelon

fresh lime juice to taste

¼ cup (2 oz/60 g) sugar, or to taste

about 2 cups (16 fl oz/500 ml) water

ice cubes

When melons are ripe and juicy, you can also make this cooling drink with cantaloupe, honeydew, or any of the numerous other varieties available at farmers' markets.

1. In a food processor, place half of the watermelon and process until smooth. Add the lime juice and half of the sugar and mix well. Refrigerate until well chilled. Pour the purée into a large pitcher. Repeat with the remaining watermelon, lime juice, and sugar and add to the pitcher. Stir well and add water to thin to the desired consistency. Taste and adjust with more sugar or lime juice if needed.

2. Serve in glasses over ice cubes.

SERVES 10

Fresh Peach Sangria

Peach trees are not uncommon in Southwestern backyards. The juicy summer fruit stars here in an updated, refreshing version of the traditional Spanish wine punch.

1. To make the simple syrup, in a saucepan over high heat, combine the sugar and water. Bring to a boil and let boil for 3 minutes, then remove from the heat and let cool. In a large pitcher or punch bowl, combine the simple syrup, wine, brandy, lemon juice, peaches, strawberries, and blueberries, if using. Stir to combine well.

2. Serve in glasses over ice cubes, garnished with a mint sprig.

SERVES 12

SIMPLE SYRUP

1¼ cups (10 oz/315 g) sugar

1¼ cups (10 fl oz/310 ml) water

1 bottle (3 cups/24 fl oz/750 ml) sparkling white wine, chilled

⅓–½ cup (3–4 fl oz/80–125 ml) peach brandy

⅓ cup (3 fl oz/80 ml) fresh lemon juice, or to taste

4 cups (1½ lb/750 g) pitted, peeled, and sliced ripe peaches

2 cups (8 oz/250 g) strawberries, stems removed and sliced

1 cup (4 oz/125 g) blueberries (optional)

ice cubes

1 bunch fresh mint

Mexican Hot Chocolate

4 cups (32 fl oz/1 l) milk

3 canela or cinnamon sticks

1 vanilla bean, split lengthwise

1 cake (2 oz/60 g) Mexican chocolate

3 oz (90 g) bittersweet chocolate

¼ cup (¾ oz/20 g) unsweetened cocoa powder

½ cup (4 fl oz/125 ml) heavy (double) cream, lightly whipped

freshly ground canela or ground cinnamon

1. In a saucepan, combine the milk and canela or cinnamon sticks. Scrape the seeds from the vanilla bean into the pan, then add the pods. Bring just to a boil, then remove from the heat and let steep for 20 minutes.

2. Add the chocolates and cocoa to the milk and warm over low heat for about 5 minutes to melt the chocolates, whisking occasionally. Remove from the heat. Discard the vanilla pods and canela sticks.

3. Transfer to a blender and process on high speed until thick and foamy, about 1 minute. Divide among 6 mugs and garnish with whipped cream and ground canela. Serve at once.

SERVES 6

Lemon Verbena Tisane

I can easily imagine herbal infusions being made to soothe body and soul on cold evenings by pioneers heading for the Southwest along the old Santa Fe Trail. This upscale version, made from dried lavender flowers, dried fruit, and lemon verbena, is delicious served plain or sweetened with a spoonful of mild honey. You can also enjoy it chilled.

7 cups (56 fl oz/1.75 l) water

¼ cup (¾ oz/20 g) dried lavender flowers

½ cup (3 oz/90 g) dried sour cherries

1 cup (1½ oz/45 g) very coarsely chopped fresh lemon verbena or lemon balm

2 cups (6 oz/185 g) packed dried apples

4 fresh tarragon sprigs

1 tablespoon coriander seed, toasted (page 141)

1. In a large saucepan, bring the water to a boil. Add the lavender flowers, cherries, lemon verbena or lemon balm, apples, tarragon, and coriander seed. Return to a boil, remove from the heat, cover, and let steep for 30 minutes.

2. Strain and serve in cups warm or chilled.

SERVES 6

Glossary

Avocado, Haas

Native to Central and South America, the avocado was brought to the Southwest centuries ago by the Spanish, and it continues to be a defining ingredient of the cuisine, whether sliced as a garnish, chopped for adding to salad, or mashed with lime juice, chiles, onion, and cilantro to make guacamole. Of the several varieties of avocado found for sale in markets, the Haas (sometimes spelled Hass), distinguished by its somewhat smaller size, tapered neck, and dark, pebbly skin, is thought to have the richest flavor and most buttery consistency. An avocado is ripe when it yields to gentle finger pressure. To peel and pit it, use a sharp knife to cut around the entire length of the fruit down to its pit. Then grasp each half in one hand and twist in opposite directions to separate the halves. The pit will remain lodged in one of them. To remove the pit, strike it firmly with the sharp edge of the knife, then twist and lift out, all the while keeping your fingers safely clear of the blade. Alternatively, scoop out the pit with a spoon. Depending on the recipe, use a spoon to scoop out the flesh from the tough skin of each half, or peel away the skin in strips and then slice or chop as required.

Bell Peppers

Roasting softens and sweetens the flesh of bell peppers (capsicums) while also loosening their skin to facilitate peeling. To roast, peel, and seed bell peppers, follow the instructions given for chiles (see below).

Capon

A male chicken castrated at a young age and allowed to grow into a plump, broad-breasted bird usually weighing 5 to 8 pounds (2.5 to 4 kg) and ideal for roasting.

Carne Adobada

Meat slowly braised in a highly seasoned sauce that typically includes garlic, onion, cumin, chile, and other seasonings. The term *adobada* comes from the traditional practice of using a spice mixture for pickling or preserving meat.

Chayote

This native squash of Central America is found outside the Southwest under a wide diversity of names, including mirliton, christophine, chocho, and vegetable pear. The last name fairly describes the shape of the squash, which is also distinguished by pale green ridged skin. The flesh, which resembles a cucumber in taste and texture, surrounds a large, flat seed that is also edible. In season from autumn to midspring, chayotes may be baked or steamed whole or halved, plain or stuffed, or may be cut up and simmered, sautéed, or fried. Young chayotes with tender skin do not require peeling.

Chiles, Roasting Fresh

Roasting develops the flavor of fresh chiles and makes removing their slightly bitter skins easier. To roast chiles, use metal tongs to hold them over the flame of a gas-stove burner until their skins blacken and blister on all sides, about 5 minutes. Alternatively, roast them on the grill rack of a hot gas or charcoal grill, or place them under a preheated broiler (griller). In both cases, turn them occasionally until evenly blackened and blistered, about 10 minutes. Using the tongs, slip the roasted chiles into a paper or heavy-duty plastic bag, or place in a heatproof bowl and cover with a heavy kitchen towel. Leave to cool for about 5 minutes, during which time the steam will help loosen the skins further. With your fingertips, peel away the skins. If the chile is to be left whole, slit carefully along the length, leaving the stem intact, and, with your fingertips, a small spoon, and/or the tip of a small, sharp knife, remove the seeds and white ribs or veins. If the chile is to be cut up, cut or pull away the stem, slit length-wise, lay the chile flat, remove the seeds and ribs, and then cut as directed. Caution: Chiles contain essential oils that can cause a painful burning sensation on contact with cuts, eyes, or other sensitive areas. Handle chiles carefully, wearing rubber kitchen gloves if you have particularly sensitive skin. After handling, wash hands, gloves, and utensils thoroughly with warm, soapy water.

Chili Sauce

This mild-flavored bottled sauce, made from tomatoes, sugar, vinegar, herbs, and spices such as chili powder or chiles, has the consistency of ketchup and is typically used as a table condiment and occasionally in cooking to flavor dishes such as beans.

Chorizo

Flavored with ground red chile, garlic, oregano, and cumin, this fresh, coarse-textured Mexican-style pork sausage adds rich, spicy flavor to many savory Southwestern dishes, from *chiles rellenos* to empanadas. Look for good-quality chorizo, in bulk or in casings, in Latin American markets. If unavailable, substitute top-of-the line spicy Polish kielbasa or Cajun andouille. If using bulk sausage, judiciously adding a little of the above-mentioned seasonings to the substitute to approximate the flavor of chorizo.

Corn Husks, Dried

Corn husks are the traditional wrappers for tamales. They hold the dough, or

masa, securely in place during cooking, and they add both a hint of their own subtle, earthy flavor and the decorative imprint of their ridged surface to the tamales. Look for stacked dried corn husks in plastic packages in Latin American markets and well-stocked food stores. Some upscale merchants now also sell carefully groomed husks that have been thoroughly inspected and cleaned, sorted, and trimmed to a uniform size.

Crema

The Mexican term for a cultured, slightly soured heavy (double) cream found in Mexican markets and well-stocked food stores. It is used as a garnish and as a sauce enrichment. The most similar and widely available substitute is the French-style cultured cream known as crème fraîche. In a pinch, substitute lightly whisked sour cream only if the cream will not be cooked, as it will curdle.

Cheeses

CHEDDAR, SHARP
Made from cow's milk, cheddar, the most popular cheese produced in the United States, comes in a range of tastes, from mild to sharp (aged) and tangy. Although not indigenous to the Southwest, its sharper versions suit the stronger flavors of the regional kitchen.

GOAT, FRESH
Smooth, white, creamy, and tangy, fresh cheeses made from goat's milk are gaining in popularity with cooks and producers throughout the United States, including a handful of small-scale cheese makers in the Southwest.

MONTEREY JACK
Named for a late-19th-century businessman in Monterey, California, who began producing this smooth, mild, semisoft cow's milk cheese, Monterey jack has become a common substitute for similar traditional cheeses produced in Mexico.

QUESO AÑEJO
Literally "aged cheese," this mature version of fresh Mexican-style cow's milk cheese (see *queso fresco,* below) is used in the Southwest, as it is in Mexico, crumbled as a garnish for tacos, enchiladas, and other foods. Grated pecorino cheese may be substituted.

QUESO FRESCO
Made from cow's milk, this "fresh cheese" of Mexico, also produced north of the border, is appreciated for its soft, somewhat crumbly consistency and salty, fresh yet tangy flavor. It may be sliced or crumbled as an ingredient that cooks in a dish or added at the end as a garnish. Mild feta cheese may be substituted.

Garlic

This member of the onion family is an indispensable ingredient in the Southwest kitchen. For the strongest garlic flavor, seek out heads of purple or red-tinged garlic, varieties popular in Mexico. Brief toasting deepens its flavor while tempering its pungency. Place unpeeled whole cloves on a hot, dry, heavy frying pan or griddle and cook for several minutes, turning frequently, until the skins are evenly charred. When the cloves are cool enough to handle, the peels will slip off easily.

Hot-Pepper Sauces

Shelves in supermarkets, Latin American markets, and specialty-food stores alike display ever-increasing numbers of hot-pepper sauces manufactured in the Southwest, the South, other parts of the United States, Mexico, the Caribbean, and elsewhere. Made by blending, distilling, and preserving various types of hot chiles, they range from mild to ferociously hot and from sharp to full bodied. Read label descriptions and sample several varieties to find those that suit your taste.

Jicama

Native to Mexico and to parts of Central and South America, and now widely available in supermarkets, this large, bulbous tuber is enjoyed for its crisp, refreshingly juicy, snowy white flesh, which has a mild, slightly sweet taste. Once the thick, fibrous brown skin is peeled away, jicama is cut into sticks or wedges for eating as a snack with a squeeze of lime and a sprinkling of salt or chile; or it is chopped, diced, or shredded for inclusion in salads.

Lard

Rendered pork fat, commonly known as lard, is a popular medium for frying in the Southwest, imparting rich, full flavor to refried beans, traditional deep-fried breads, and other foods. Look for good-quality lard rendered by a butcher; it will have a flavor superior to that of packaged processed lard sold in food stores.

Lime

Southwest cooks prefer the small, round, sometimes yellow-tinged lime known by Mexican cooks as *lima*. It has a sharper, fuller flavor than the larger, sweeter-tasting, more common Persian lime.

Oils

Several different kinds of oil are used to cook or season foods in the Southwest kitchen. Flavorless safflower oil and vegetable oil are common cooking oils. One of the most popular oils, particularly among contemporary cooks, is olive oil. Extra-virgin olive oil, extracted from the first pressing without use of heat or chemicals, will have the best flavor. Look in specialty-food stores for seasoning oils based on olive oil, such as lemon-, lime-, or orange-flavored olive oil. Two other widespread seasoning oils are deep brown oil pressed from toasted

Herbs

CILANTRO

Also called Chinese parsley and fresh coriander, this bright-tasting, pungent herb resembles flat-leafed (Italian) parsley in appearance only. It is a common ingredient in salsas and sauces and a popular garnish.

EPAZOTE

These slender, pointed, sawtooth-edged leaves, also known as wormseed, Mexican tea, and goosefoot, have a pungent flavor sometimes likened to camphor. Used both fresh (easily grown from seed) and dried, epazote is an essential ingredient in bean cookery, complementing the earthiness of the legumes while also reputedly reducing the gastric distress caused by them.

HOJA SANTA

Large and heart shaped, this green "sacred leaf," a common seasoning in Mexico, has a taste resembling those of sassafras and licorice. Also known as *hierba santa*, it is used primarily to season sauces and as a wrapper for steamed foods and is believed to aid digestion.

MINT

This refreshing herb has a wide range of uses, flavoring savory ingredients such as lamb along with beverages and desserts.

OREGANO, MEXICAN

Mexican varieties of this popular herb tend to have a more pronounced flavor than other varieties. Look for dried whole leaf oregano in Mexican markets and, as with any dried herb, crush it in your palm with your thumb to help release its essential oils just before adding it to a dish.

peanuts and deep green oil pressed from toasted pumpkin seeds. Look for these oils in specialty-food stores, health-food stores, and Latin American markets.

Onions
Southwest cooks add onions to salsas and guacamole, tacos and enchiladas, soups and stews. The two most commonly used types are the strong-tasting white-skinned onion favored in Mexico and the sweeter-tasting red (Spanish) onion.

Panko
Japanese dried bread crumbs, which are larger than conventional Western dried crumbs and have jagged edges, are usually packed in cellophane bags. Look for them in Japanese markets and well-stocked food stores.

Panocha Flour
This finely milled flour, sometimes labeled *harina para panocha,* is ground from sprouted wheat and is used in the Southwest to make a traditional Native American pudding known as *panocha.* Whole-wheat flour may be substituted.

Purslane
Resembling slightly elongated leaves of watercress, this mild, succulent green, eaten both raw and cooked, is also known by the Spanish *verdolagas* and the Hopi *peehala.* In the Southwest, it is traditionally gathered in the wild, but it may also be grown at home or found in well-stocked greengrocers or farmers' markets.

Salt, Kosher
Free of additives, this coarse-grained salt is only about half as salty as common table salt when added in the same amount. Its texture is a welcome addition to some dishes.

Spices, Toasting and Grinding
To bring out the full flavor of spices, such as coriander and cumin seeds, purchase them whole and toast and grind them at home, preparing only what you need at the time. To toast them, put the seeds in a dry, heavy frying pan over medium heat and warm them until they are fragrant and just begin to change color, shaking the pan as necessary to prevent scorching. This should take only a few minutes. Pour onto a plate, let cool, then grind in a spice grinder or with a mortar and pestle.

Squash Blossoms
The delicate blooms of zucchini and other squashes that grow in the Southwest are popular ingredients, adding golden color and subtle taste and texture to quesadillas and salads. They are also deep-fried, either plain or stuffed. Look for the blossoms in well-stocked food stores and farmers' markets in the summer squash season, or grow your own, ideally picking them in the morning when they have just opened. Use as soon as possible after harvest or purchase.

Tamarind Concentrate
The dark reddish brown pulp found inside the pods of the tropical tamarind tree has a tangy sweet-sour flavor that complements both savory and sweet dishes. Ethnic markets sell the pods loose or the pulp in blocks or concentrate form. The latter, sold in small jars, is the easiest to use.

Tequila, Gold
Fermented and distilled from the juice of the blue agave cactus, this signature spirit of Mexico is available under many brands. All tequila must contain at least 51 percent spirit from blue agave, which is combined with other forms of alcohol.

Mexican government regulations do not specify aging for gold tequilas, but the better ones are aged at least a couple of months in oak and are smoother than unaged white (silver) tequilas. Gold tequilas get their color from the addition of caramel. They are not, however, as rich or complex as aged *(añejo)* tequilas, which are kept in oak for at least a year.

Tomatillos
Members of the gooseberry family, these fruits look like small green tomatoes covered in papery brown husks. The husks are usually removed as the first step in the fruits' preparation. Tomatillos may be used raw or cooked in salsas and other savory preparations. Look for fresh ones in Latin American markets, some farmers' markets, and in well-stocked food stores. They are also available canned.

Tomatoes, Roma
Also known as plum or egg tomatoes, these oval, meaty tomatoes offer consistently good flavor and texture year-round.

Vinegars
Vinegar can be made from any alcoholic beverage that undergoes a secondary fermentation, turning its alcohol to acid. It is used for everything from salad dressings to sauces to seasonings, and good-quality vinegars will convey the flavor qualities of the beverage from which they are derived. Among the vinegars well suited to Southwestern cooking are cider vinegar, which imparts the sweet, fruity flavor of apples; rich, woody sherry vinegar, based on the Spanish (or Spanish-style) fortified wine of the same name; and crisp, clean-tasting white wine vinegar.

Index

Acknowledgments

Mil gracias to Barbara Kafka from Kathi Long.

Leigh Beisch wishes to thank Jory Winery, Phipps Country Beans, and Tierra Vegetables.

Weldon Owen wishes to thank the following people and associations for their generous assistance and support in producing this book:
Desne Border, Ken DellaPenta, Dana Goldberg, Chris Hemesath, Annette Sandoval, and Hill Nutrition Associates.

Photo Credits

Weldon Owen wishes to thank the following photographers and organizations for permission to reproduce their copyrighted photographs:
(Clockwise from top left) Pages 14–15 : Melanie Acevedo, Laurie Smith, Rob Howard, Lisa Romerein, Erik Rank, Caroyl La Barge, Paul Slaughter
Page 16: Lisa Romerein, Lois Ellen Frank, Rob Howard, Martyn Thompson, Evan Sklar
Page 44: Paul Slaughter, Rob Howard, Rob Howard, Sheri Giblin, Laurie Smith
Page 82: Lois Ellen Frank, Ellen Silverman, Lois Ellen Frank, Amy Haskell, Caroline Kopp, Evan Sklar
Page 118: Laurie Smith, Evan Sklar, Caren Alpert, Scott Warren, Sheri Giblin

Time-Life Books is a division of Time Life Inc.

Time-Life is a trademark of Time Warner Inc.,

and affiliated companies.

TIME LIFE INC.

President and CEO: **Jim Nelson**

TIME-LIFE TRADE PUBLISHING

Vice President and Publisher: **Neil Levin**

Vice President, Content Development:

Jennifer L. Pearce

WILLIAMS-SONOMA

Founder and Vice-Chairman: **Chuck Williams**

Book Buyer: **Cecilia Michaelis**

WELDON OWEN INC.

Chief Executive Officer: **John Owen**

President: **Terry Newell**

Chief Operating Officer: **Larry Partington**

Vice President International Sales: **Stuart Laurence**

Associate Publisher: **Val Cipollone**

Editor: **Sarah Lemas**

Copy Editor: **Sharon Silva**

Consulting Editor: **Norman Kolpas**

Design: **Jane Palecek**

Production Director: **Stephanie Sherman**

Food Stylist: **George Dolese**

Prop Stylist: **Sara Slavin**

Studio Assistant: **Sheri Giblin**

Food Styling Assistant: **Leslie Busch**

Scenic Photo Research: **Caren Alpert**

The Williams-Sonoma New American Cooking Series
conceived and produced by Weldon Owen Inc.
814 Montgomery Street, San Francisco, CA 94133

In collaboration with Williams-Sonoma
3250 Van Ness Avenue, San Francisco, CA 94109

Separations by Bright Arts Graphics (S) Pte. Ltd.
Printed in Singapore by Tien Wah Press (Pte.) Ltd.

A WELDON OWEN PRODUCTION

First printed in 2001
10 9 8 7 6 5 4 3 2 1

Library of Congress
Cataloging-in-Publication Data

Long, Kathi.
The Southwest / general editor, Chuck Williams; recipes and
text, Kathi Long; photography, Leigh Beisch.
    p. cm. — (Williams-Sonoma New American Cooking)
    Includes index.
    ISBN 0-7370-2047-4
    1. Cookery, American--Southwestern style. I. Williams,
Chuck. II. Title. III. Series.
TX715.2.S69 L66   2001
641.5979— dc21   00-064826
                                   CIP

A NOTE ON NUTRITIONAL ANALYSIS
Each recipe is analyzed for significant nutrients per
serving. Not included in the analysis are ingredients
that are optional or added to taste, or are suggested
as an alternative or substitution either in the recipe
or in the recipe introduction. In recipes that yield
a range of servings, the analysis is for the middle
of that range.

A NOTE ON WEIGHTS AND MEASURES
All recipes include customary U.S. and metric
measurements. Metric conversions are based on
a standard developed for these books and have
been rounded off. Actual weights may vary.